A DISAPPEARING NUMBER

Complicite

A Disappearing Number

Conceived and directed by Simon McBurney

Devised by the Company

OBERON BOOKS
LONDON

First published in 2008 by Oberon Books Ltd
521 Caledonian Road, London N7 9RH
Tel: 020 7607 3637 / Fax: 020 7607 3629
e-mail: info@oberonbooks.com
www.oberonbooks.com

Reprinted in 2009

Cover photographs by Robbie Jack.

Plate section photographs by Sarah Ainslie.

ISBN: 978-1-84002-830-0

Printed in Great Britain by Antony Rowe Ltd, Chippenham.

Contents

*An eight-page plate section of rehearsal
photographs from the 2007 production of
A Disappearing Number can be found between
pages 32 and 33. All photographs are by Sarah Ainslie.*

Introduction

I look out of the window into the dark. I am flying to Chennai.
Madras. Below me is darkness too. I wonder if it is desert and
realise I have no idea where we are. I sometimes like the way
flying anaesthetises all sense of place. No one can contact you;
you do not belong in the air, and strangely you sense you do not
belong anywhere. As a result flying is a time of remembering and
imagining. So I lean back and wonder where to begin with this
show. Where do I start? When Ramanujan wrote to Hardy from
Madras in 1913 he was forbidden to make the *reverse* journey I
am making now. His Brahmin caste wouldn't allow it. And so,
the story goes, he went to the great temple at Namakkal, south
of his home town Kombakonam, and waited for a sign. The story
is nothing without the mathematical ideas, I'm thinking, and
I am no mathematician. 'Mathematicians are only makers of
patterns, like poets or painters', said Hardy in *A Mathematician's
Apology*. So perhaps I should simply make a set of patterns. But
even a mathematician's patterns are made of ideas and so far I
have none.

I know that many artists work in the dark not knowing where
to begin until they do. There is always a leap into the unknown
not yet taken and we wait for an idea to come, for a sense of the
structure of the story or drama, any sign would do, for someone
to tell you something.

'There are countable infinities and uncountable infinities', said
Marcus du Sautoy, the mathematician who is collaborating with
us for this piece, and I thought he was taking the piss.

    'And some infinities are bigger than others,' added Victoria
Gould, our other mathematician who is also an actress.

    What are you talking about? Surely that is just an unproven
idea. How can some infinities be bigger than others?

    They can.

    I look at Marcus's blue eyes and believe him as he begins to
show us how.

On hot summer evenings when I was about six, my parents would lay out an ancient canvas groundsheet in the garden. My brother, sister and I would run to get our sleeping bags, lie on our backs and gaze up at the night sky waiting for sleep to come. The infinite became apparent in the stars. An unknown at once alarming and comforting. Alarming because there were no answers. Comforting because anything seemed possible in that mighty blackness.

Arriving at Chennai airport at 4 am I was still dreaming. Out through the mass of people a man was waiting with a sign.

'I am Ragu', he said.

We go to an old van. I sit up front as we chug out of town. People wailing everywhere, carrying branches, food, water and trays of tea, bicycles with churns tied to the back, carts, motorcycles, we drive round a cow and the holes. Flowers line the roadside like a sign saying 'this way please'. It goes on for miles, then a straggling line of people, and finally a cart being pushed.

'Funeral', says Ragu.

On the cart, wrapped in white, lies a corpse. I look into its face as we pass. The flowers were marking the way to another world.

So the square root of four is two or minus two. And the square root of two is irrational. Does that mean it is mad? No, simply that you cannot express it as a fraction. The first 25 decimal places are 1.41421 35623 73095 04880 16887…and so it goes on, into infinity. But what is the square root of minus one?

'Minus one,' someone tentatively suggests.

'Minus one times minus one is plus one.'

Ah yes.

'Well maybe there is no square root of minus one. This absolutely infuriated mathematicians because without it there were equations they could not solve. So one day some mathematician simply said "Fuck it. We need a square root of minus one, and if we imagine it, it will exist." And so they did. It was a leap of the imagination and they called it "i", the imaginary number. And this "leap" gave us complex numbers.

And without complex numbers we would not be able to describe electromagnetic behaviour or create digital technology in the way that we have. We would have no radio, no television, nor the mobile phone that you are holding in your hand.' I look at my mobile. A leap of the imagination.

Waking in the garden my heart would sink. Time for school, where I would understand nothing about maths except that I got the wrong answer. Nothing to do with the imagination. That would have to wait until art class. At no time did I make a connection between what I saw at night and the blackboard I would be staring at so soon.

Ten hours later I wake in another country. Gigantic red rocks dot the landscape. Palm trees everywhere. We are in Trichy. A small town of some seven and a half million inhabitants. I take a hotel room for a few hours and sleep. Then wake when the others arrive, my designer Michael Levine and assistant producer Polly Stokes. We cram into an ancient four-wheel drive to get to Namakkal before nightfall. We stop on the banks of the Cauvery. We stand looking out at this 'Ganges' of the south. Somewhere there is supposed to be an underground link between the two rivers. All who bathe in her are cleansed of their sins.

Two men are slowly making their way to the water. They lay out their washing things on the stones beside the river, soap, leaves, a clean dhoti. With three deft movements they change their dhotis with their backs to us, then stand one foot in, one out of the water and wash the other cloth in the river. Having wrung them out, they leisurely swing them against the rocks lining the bank. Then they both slowly, very slowly, slide into the water and immerse themselves up to their necks.

When we enter Namakkal all is dark, lit by candle and oil.
'A black out', says our driver.
The name Namakkal derives from Namagiri, which is the name of the single rock formation at the centre of the town. It is enormous, of granite, 65 metres high and more than a kilometre in circumference. Over it is a fort. It is called Tippu Sultan's fort. The front gates are five metres high and four across. Closing time

is near and we slip in past three kneeling women on the steps, our hands sliding over the carvings of the thick wooden door, leave our shoes at the entrance and walk inside. A wide, open space, there are pillars and rectangular temples. The residual heat from the day warms our palms as we press them against the walls. It creeps up from the rough stone ground under our soles.

Here Ramanujan slept for three days and nights in 1913. 'Normally all leave at dusk, but he was allowed to sleep here', said our guide. I try to see him there in the soft dark. The air here embraces you like a blanket.

We turn into the temple. We walk up beside a sacred walkway. Suddenly there are priests. We are given water, a mark is pressed onto our foreheads and a bell-like object briefly placed on our heads. There are flowers floating in wooden bowls of water, and somewhere someone is singing softly. The air is heavy with incense. A bell rings, people talk, children are playing. A priest is eating his dinner while another prays.

The heat is stifling. Perhaps hotter than outside where it is still 35 degrees though night. The chanting becomes more intense, and my eyes wander to the carvings of Vishnu on the walls. In one he has taken on his multi-armed form and is ripping open the stomach of a prone woman. A child pats her leg and smiles at me as he pops something into his mouth. I smile back and wander out into the night. I find a corner of the temple where it is calm. Everything here is mysterious, but not mystical. The mysterious is part of the everyday. The unknown feels familiar.

My hands touch the rock. I put my back against it, squat and feel reassured. I have been travelling for nearly 30 hours. I gaze up at the night sky. No answer comes to me, no vision, no sign. But it is warm. And I feel more at home than I have done for ages. Suddenly it seems clear that it is here where Ramanujan should have found the courage to look beyond the strictures of Brahmin law – knowing he would suffer total rejection from his caste, his friends, neighbours, family – and decide to travel to England. Here where the unknown is so recognisable. And all he did was wait. For the courage to emerge out of the warm rock. So I look at the stars and wait.

'Where did it all begin? How big is it? Surely it must have an end, an edge?' I would ask my brother, leaning over as I was going to sleep, so he would talk and I could drift away on the back of his voice.

'So what was there before the beginning?' I ask.

'What?'

'When did it all really begin?'

My brother sighs. He is only nine but he sighs.

I roll onto my back and wait for the answer. I gaze at the stars. And wait. And the black between the stars. And wait.

Simon McBurney
August 2007, London

A most romantic collaboration

by Marcus du Sautoy

In January 1913 the Cambridge mathematician Godfrey Harold Hardy received a strange letter in the morning post. It contained wild, fantastic theorems about prime numbers, one of the great mysteries of mathematics. Hardy nearly threw the letter in the bin – maths attracts its fair share of cranks – but by the evening the theorems were beginning to work their magic. Hardy could see that the letter was the work of a genius. What was even more intriguing was that it had come from the other side of the world. The author was a 26-year-old clerk earning 20 rupees a month in the Madras Port Authority, India. His name was Srinivasa Ramanujan.

There was one formula in particular that struck a chord with Hardy. To the uninitiated it seemed to make no sense at all:

$$1+2+3+4+5+... = -\frac{1}{12}$$

Indeed, Ramanujan had already sent his letter to a number of mathematicians, who had rejected the Indian's ideas as the work of a madman. But it was this very formula that provided Hardy with his first inkling that Ramanujan was far from a crank. Hardy knew that there were sophisticated mathematical techniques developed in Germany that had once made sense of these infinite sums but they were not ideas that had spread widely. Hardy realised that Ramanujan must have single-handedly reconstructed them.

It is this same formula that has provided a catalyst for Complicite's investigation of Ramanujan's relationship with Hardy and, more generally, the company's exploration of the mathematical world. What is the mysterious journey behind adding up all the whole numbers and getting the answer minus one twelfth? How does one make sense of the concept of infinity? What does it mean to say there are many different types of infinity? Why are the primes fundamental yet so deeply mysterious to mathematicians? What constitutes a mathematical pattern against the chaos that pervades so much of the physical world? What is mathematical proof?

This last concept of proof is especially relevant to the relationship between the two mathematicians. Hardy persuaded Ramanujan to break with his Brahmin beliefs, which forbade travel across the seas, and to join him in Cambridge. Together they journeyed like Edmund Hillary and Tenzing Norgay across the mathematical wilds. It was not an easy collaboration, however. While Hardy insisted on the rigours of western ideas of proof, Ramanujan's theorems were spilling from his mind thanks, he claimed, to the inspiration of his goddess Namagiri.

Ramanujan relied on an extraordinary mathematical intuition to make connections between seemingly unrelated ideas. Hardy noted: 'It seemed ridiculous to worry him about how he had found this or that known theorem, when he was showing me half a dozen new ones almost every day'. It was often up to Hardy to supply the rigorous proofs that would be expected by the western journals to which they submitted their papers. It was a real culture clash, like trying to marry the traditions of western classical music with the ragas and talas of India.

This tension between east and west is one that runs throughout much of mathematical history. For many like Hardy, mathematics was regarded as a European endeavour dating back to the traditions of Ancient Greece. The influence of other cultures has received little recognition. But many of the great mathematical ideas, such as the concept of zero and the potency of infinite sums, have their origins in India. This confrontation is at the heart of Complicite's production.

Ramanujan returned to India after the end of the First World War. Tragically he died shortly after his arrival from a parasitic infection of the liver. Hardy was devastated. He regarded their collaboration as the one romantic incident of his life. But perhaps more remarkable was the mathematics contained in the last letter that Ramanujan sent to Hardy in 1920.

It was full of talk of a new mathematical idea he called a mock theta function and it was way ahead of its time. Only in the past few years has a full understanding of Ramanujan's functions become clear: Kathrin Bringmann and Ken Ono of the University of Wisconsin have given the first complete explanation of the ideas contained in that last letter.

It is striking in a world dominated by men that a woman has been a key character in illuminating Ramanujan's work. Complicite's production also places a woman at the centre of its fascinating mathematical story.

But the mock theta function is not the only idea to live on long after Ramanujan's death. His work on modular forms, for example, has become key to making sense of string theory, currently being proposed by physicists to explain the universe. As Hardy once wrote: 'Immortality may be a silly word, but probably a mathematician has the best chance of whatever it may mean.' Ramanujan's work during the three decades he was alive seems to straddle generations of mathematical ideas. His first letter to Hardy reconstructed the mathematics of nineteenth-century Germany. His last letter was the catalyst for ideas that still resonate today. Like two bookends, these letters encompass three centuries of modern mathematics.

Marcus du Sautoy is a Professor of Mathematics
at Wadham College, Oxford. His book
The Music of the Primes *(HarperPerennial)*
describes Ramanujan's and Hardy's impact
on the story of prime numbers.

A Disappearing Number was co-produced by Complicite, barbicanbite07, Wiener Festwochen, Holland Festival and Ruhrfestspiele Recklinghausen, in association with Theatre Royal Plymouth. It was first performed at the Theatre Royal Plymouth on 28 March 2007 and revived in 2008.

This is the version of the play as performed at the Barbican Theatre, London, in September 2007.

Complicite
A DISAPPEARING NUMBER
Conceived and Directed by Simon McBurney
Devised by the Company

Directed by	Simon McBurney
Original Music	Nitin Sawhney
Design	Michael Levine
Lighting	Paul Anderson
Sound	Christopher Shutt
Projection	Sven Ortel for mesmer
Costume	Christina Cunningham
Cast	David Annen
	Firdous Bamji
	Paul Bhattacharjee
	Hiren Chate
	Saraj Chaudhry
	Divya Kasturi
	Chetna Pandya
	Saskia Reeves
	Shane Shambhu
Associate Director	Catherine Alexander
Literary Associate	Ben Power
Artistic Collaborator	Victoria Gould
Artistic Associate	Annie Castledine

Production Manager	Katrina Gilroy
Company Stage Manager	Cath Binks
Technical Stage Manager	Rod Wilson
Deputy Stage Manager	Perrine Desproges
Assistant Stage Manager	Ian Andlaw
Associate Sound	Kay Basson
Associate Projection	Finn Ross
Projection Technician	Tim Perrett
Projection Electrician	Dan Lloyd
Wardrobe Mistress	Donna Richards
Assistant to the Director	Amelia Hashemi
Costume Supervisor	Poppy Hall
Assistant Design	James Humphrey
Research	Jess Gormley
Maths Consultant	Marcus du Sautoy
Producer	Judith Dimant
Assistant Producer	Polly Stokes
Education and Marketing	Natasha Freedman
Assistant to the Producer	Chip Horne
Administrator	Anita Ashwick
Administrative Assistant	Fiona Stewart

and thanks to Elayce Ismail and Sharon Kwan

A Disappearing Number is in part inspired by G H Hardy's
A Mathematician's Apology with foreword by C P Snow.
Complicite would like to thank Cambridge University Press
for granting permission to use material from these texts in the
production.

Founded in 1983 and led by Simon McBurney, Complicite's
work ranges from devised work to theatrical adaptations and
revivals of classic texts as well as work in radio and film.

www.complicite.org

A note on the text

A Disappearing Number is a play whose fluidity and use of video, movement, music and sound design, in addition to text, make it largely resistant to attempts to capture and pin down in traditional script form. What follows should be regarded as a record of Complicite's original production, although there are a number of technical elements which are not annotated here.

The time-structures of the play are, at times, deliberately ambiguous. The idea of exploring two or more time-schemes simultaneously was crucial to the development of the piece. Roughly speaking, the 'present' is the night which Al spends locked in the Brunel University lecture hall and his subsequent visit to India. The 'past' mostly spans the years between 1913 and 1919, in the case of the Ramanujan / Hardy narrative, and the five years leading up to the 'present' in the case of Al and Ruth. There are also moments which are outside these periods. The script attempts to make this clear.

Ben Power – Literary Associate
March 2008

1

A university lecture hall, with a large whiteboard in the centre. To one side, a desk and an overhead projector; to the other side, a door and a portable lectern. On the wall close to the door is a telephone.

AL stands next to the desk with his back to the audience. RUTH enters. She writes '1, 2, 3, 4, 5' on the whiteboard.

RUTH: (*Nervous.*) Good evening ladies and gentlemen. I'd like to go through one or two very basic mathematical ideas that are integral to this evening so that the recurrent mathematical themes become clear to you all.

Right, OK. (*Beat.*) Let's consider these sets of numbers. (*She writes them up as she speaks.*) 2, 4, 6, 8, 10...2, 3, 5, 7, 11...1, 2, 4, 8, 16... These are known as sequences, and they have two characteristics. The terms can go on forever and they have a pattern, which helps you to continue the sequence. Some patterns are more obvious than others. With these numbers (*Indicates the first sequence.*) the pattern is very clear. But in this sequence, (*Indicates the second sequence.*) the primes, the pattern is less obvious. Is there a pattern at all? To find the hidden pattern you sometimes need to look at them in a new way. If we add together the terms of a sequence, we would have what is known in mathematics as a series. (*She writes four '+'s between the numbers.*)

So, $1+2+4+8+16$ is a finite series with 5 terms, with the sum of 31. If we allow the series to continue forever, it would become an infinite series. And it is clear that the sum of: $1+2+4+8+16$ and so on to infinity is itself infinite, making it a *divergent* series. That is to say it diverges from zero, that is to say the difference between the sum and zero widens infinitely.

(*She writes the maths up as she speaks.*) I can also express the above series as the sum of integral powers of 2. 2 to the power of 0 plus 2 to the power of 1 plus 2 squared plus 2 cubed plus 2 to the power of 4 plus... Or using the sigma notation of a sum we can write it another way: 'the sum from r equals zero to infinity of 2 to the power of r.'

I would like to show you another divergent series, perhaps the simplest of all: 1+2+3+4+...and so on to infinity equals infinity. All of this is very logical. Now I'm going to do something very strange. I'm going to disrupt our sense of logic and I'm going to show you something really thrilling.

1+2+3+4+5+ and so on to infinity equals minus one twelfth. (*Beat.*) 'How can this be?' And you'd be right to think so! But let me show you how one can obtain this anomalous result using the Functional Equation of the Riemann Zeta Function. And this is how it goes...

RUTH begins to write out the Functional Equation of the Riemann Zeta Function (see Appendix). The maths gets quicker and more complicated.

2 to the power of 1 minus Z, times the gamma of Z, times the zeta of Z, times the cosine of a half pi Z, is equal to pi to the power of Z, times the zeta of 1 minus Z. This is only true for complex values of z. Where z equals x plus i y, where i is the square root of minus 1 – our imaginary number.

The gamma of z is a very well known definition. The gamma of z is equal to the integral from 0 to infinity of e to the minus t times t to the power of z minus 1 with respect to t. For complex z this is equal to z minus 1 factorial.

Enter ANINDA RAO. He watches RUTH.

The zeta of z equals the sum from n equals 1 to infinity of 1 over n to the power of z. I'm going to put the value 2 into this equation (For which, remember, it is not defined) and then I will show you what happens.

2 to the power of 1 minus 2, times the gamma of 2, times the zeta of 2, times the cosine of a half pi times 2. A half of 2 is 1 so we have the cosine of just pi is equal to pi squared, times the zeta of 1 minus 2...

RUTH continues to lecture, oblivious, as ANINDA addresses the audience.

ANINDA: (*In an Indian accent.*) You're probably wondering at this point if this is the entire show. I'm Aninda, this is Al and this is Ruth. (*Pause. His accent changes.*) Actually, that's a lie. I'm an actor playing Aninda, he's an actor playing Al and she's an actress playing Ruth. But the mathematics is real. It's terrifying, but it's real.

When I was a child I had a real problem with mathematics. I remember I had a chart on the back of my door. It went, '1 – One Tractor'. '2 – Two Pineapples'. And, for a reason that nobody could explain, there were three medicine bottles. Then, four pears...and five oranges. Of course when they added one plus two equals three, I tried to understand how one tractor plus two pineapples could make three medicine bottles. (*Beat.*) They'd talk about five oranges, which was fine, but when they took away the oranges, that's when the problems began. As I got older they replaced the numbers with letters – a, b, c...x, y, z. So just to walk into a maths class would bring me out in a cold sweat. That's when I thought I had a problem with abstract thinking, but I had no problem with other imaginary ideas. In the school playground I would pretend to be the headmaster of my primary school, Mr Stoddart. I'd do this (*He strikes a silly pose.*) and the other children would laugh. Of course, I wasn't really Mr Stoddart, I was PRETENDING to be Mr Stoddart. (*Beat.*) But I still had a problem with the idea that this (*Indicates the maths.*) is real. In fact we could say that this is the only real thing here.

(*He approaches RUTH, who is still lecturing.*) Just to prove to you that we are in the imaginary world of the theatre, I'll take her glasses. (*He lifts the glasses off her face, puts his fingers through the eye holes.*) There's no glass in there! Bloody useless! Even her voice can be changed...all I have to do is this. (*He fiddles with an imaginary dial and RUTH's voice becomes ridiculously high-pitched.*) Now the maths is even more mystifying! Of course I'm not actually doing this, it's the sound man up there. (*He indicates the box at the back of the auditorium.*) Everything is fake BUT the mathematics. (*He picks up a phone, attached to the wall.*) This phone for example… 'Hello mum?'… no mum, no ring tone! (*He pushes the door open.*) This door doesn't lead anywhere! I can push these walls right off! (*He pushes the wall which gracefully slides offstage. The other walls do likewise. A dark void is revealed behind. A MUSICIAN walks onstage and takes a seat with his tablas to one side.*) This is Hiren Chate. He is real and he will really play the real tablas.

And now, I can do what I could never do at school. I can put my hands on this board and push… (*He pushes the whiteboard, which flies up and offstage.*)…and now I've got rid of the maths! (*Beat. RUTH produces a piece of chalk and continues to write on a black screen which has been revealed behind the whiteboard.*) She has a piece of chalk! So if I really want to get rid of the maths I have to get rid of the mathematician. (*He rotates the screen and RUTH disappears through it.*) We have finally got rid of the mathematics.

(*Pause. ANINDA reverts to his Indian accent.*) But of course we haven't. Because mathematics is everywhere. (*Beat.*) I am Aninda Rao. I'm a physicist. I specialise in string theory. For those of you who do not have a working knowledge of string theory, I will quote Spike Milligan… 'String is a very important thing. Rope is thicker, but string is quicker'. (*He points at AL.*) This is Al. In temporal terms he is in the present. That was Ruth, she's in the past and I am giving a lecture in CERN, in Switzerland…about a year ago.

(*He looks out at the audience.*) They say mathematics is not a spectator sport, so please think of a number. Don't tell anyone, this is your own personal, secret, number. We will call this number 'n'. Unless you are like Daniel Tammet and can remember pi to twenty-two thousand decimal places, please choose a simple number. (*Beat.*) Now multiply that number by two. (*Beat.*) Now add fourteen. (*He points into the auditorium.*) Someone is already with their head in their hands – obviously choosing a negative number has repercussions. Now divide this new number in two. (*Beat.*) Finally, take away your original number. (*Pause.*) And what I like about the theatre is that we are all able to imagine the same thing at the same time, just as now, we are all imagining the number seven.

(*Pause.*) Now I want you to imagine that Al is in India, and this plastic chair is a taxi in Madras.

The MUSICIAN begins to play. Enter a DRIVER. ANINDA and AL sit on two plastic chairs, AL carrying a red suitcase. On the screen we see Chennai. Traffic screeches past them.

ANINDA: (*To DRIVER.*) …Triplicane, Triplicane. (*To AL.*) First I will take you to his house and then I'll take you to the Cauvery, the river where he spent much of his time. Have you really never been to India before?

AL: We went to Bombay once when I was five.

ANINDA: Are you enjoying it?

AL: It's a little overwhelming!

ANINDA: One thing, only drink the bottled water.

AL: OK.

The taxi stops. The DRIVER exits as ANINDA and AL stand. We see a temple behind them.

ANINDA: We are here.

ANINDA and AL step through the screen. Their silhouettes are in Chennai.

This is the temple at the end of his street.

A WOMAN enters, begging. She shouts at ANINDA in Tamil, but he brushes her away. He points AL towards the temple.

This tower you can see is called the Goporam. In one structure we can see all reality, the inter-dependence of everything. He looked at this every day of his life. It was just opposite his house from where, in 1913, he wrote his first letter to G H Hardy.

RAMANUJAN: (*Voice-over.*) Dear Sir, I beg to introduce myself to you as a clerk in the accounts department of the Port Trust Office at Madras... Please do not think me mad if I state that $1+2+3+4$ and so on to infinity is equal to minus one twelfth...

ANINDA reappears through the screen as AL freezes in Chennai.

ANINDA: This has not happened to Al yet, but it will happen, it's in the future. (*Beat.*) And now I want to go forward into the past.

ANINDA exits as Chennai disappears.

2

RUTH reappears through the screen and continues to write upon it.

RUTH: (*Mid-lecture.*) Now we can see it unfolding and see how Ramanujan arrived at this result…1 over 4 to the power of minus 1, plus 1 over 5 to the power of minus 1 and so on to infinity equals minus one twelfth. 1 to the power of minus 1 is just 1, 2 to the power of minus 1 is a half, 3 to the power of minus 1 is a third, 4 to the power of minus 1 is a quarter, 5 to the power of minus 1 is a fifth and so on to infinity equals minus one twelfth. So, half into 1 is 2, a third into 1 is 3, a quarter into 1 is 4, a fifth into 1 is 5 to infinity equals minus a twelfth.

Clearly this result looks anomalous! As G H Hardy said, 'A mathematician, like a painter, or a poet, is a maker of patterns… And beauty is the first test…' (*She points at the equation.*) Look at this in a new way and a hidden pattern emerges which connects the two sides of the equation in the most extraordinarily beautiful way. And this pattern led to one of the most remarkable relationships in the history of mathematics. And tomorrow we will go deeper into what that collaboration is about. But for now, thank you very much.

Her lecture over, RUTH prepares to leave. AL rises from a seat in the auditorium.

AL: Excuse me.

RUTH: Yes.

AL: You got a minute?

RUTH: Yes, is there a problem? You're not a student are you?

AL: No. I'm not even a mature student. I'm here by mistake.

RUTH: A very careless mistake, you were sitting in the front row yesterday. I hope you weren't too bored.

AL: I haven't understood a word you've said, but I've found it fascinating. You clearly like what you do.

RUTH: I love what I do.

AL: I want to ask you a question because yesterday you were talking about infinity.

RUTH: Yes.

AL: Infinity is something that has always frightened me.

RUTH: For mathematicians infinity is just another mathematical concept. It's no big deal.

AL: It's a big deal for me, because it's where I'm going to go when I die. (*RUTH laughs.*) You seemed to be suggesting that there was more than one infinity?

RUTH: Yes. There is an infinity of infinities.

AL: Oh shit…

RUTH: There are countable infinities and uncountable infinities. Some infinities are larger than others.

AL: You can count them?

RUTH: If you want to, but you'd die trying.

AL: That's what I'm afraid of.

RUTH: I really must go.

RUTH begins to leave.

AL: Wait! There is one particular number that I am, in fact, interested in.

RUTH: Yes?

Pause.

AL: It's your phone number.

Pause. RUTH smiles.

RUTH: I've never been asked that before. After a lecture, I mean…

AL: You're blushing.

RUTH: You're blushing.

AL: See where the Riemann Zeta Function gets you.

Pause. They are grinning at each other.

RUTH: Sorry, who are you?

AL: I'm Al Cooper. (*The sound of a plane, overhead.*) I was in the Business Ethics and Sustainability conference next door. The door was open so I just walked in…

RUTH: (*Gesturing to the sky.*) That's why we finish lecturing early. Because they've changed the flight path.

AL: I'll be on one of those the day after tomorrow. (*Beat.*) So, can I have it?

Pause. RUTH looks at him.

RUTH: Let's see. Tomorrow we go beyond the Riemann Zeta Function into what Ramanujan did next.

AL: I'll be here.

Exit RUTH. AL watches her go.

3

AL looks at the numbers on the screen.

AL: 1, 2, 3... (*He turns and stops speaking, but his voice continues to count up. He listens, then begins to count backwards.*) -1, -2, -3... (*Again, he stops speaking but his voice continues. Now there are counting voices in both directions. AL listens.*) And between 1 and 2 there is an infinity of other numbers such as 1.1 and 1.2. ...and 1.11 and 1.12...and 1.111 and 1.112... and 1.1111 and...

He stops and, again, his voice continues the pattern.

RUTH: (*Voice-over.*) There are no gaps between the numbers, like there are no gaps in time or space; they are continuous. And if time is continuous, then we are linked to the past and future. And if space is continuous we are linked to the absent.

A distant light behind the screen. RUTH enters. Projected onto the screen is the action of the forestage but with a four second delay. It gives the impression of shadows, spectres of repeating time.

AL: Ruth!

AL moves towards her and as he does so, RUTH walks past him through the screen. The company follows her, passing one at a time into the darkness. AL watches, then follows. The screen begins to rotate continuously. A YOUNG INDIAN WOMAN enters and pauses for a moment.

YOUNG WOMAN: (*Voice-over.*) I remember standing on the rail of the boat as it pulled away from India. And my parents were both crying and crying and India was getting smaller and smaller and all the lights were getting dimmer and dimmer. They were crying because they knew they would never see her again.

She moves off, through the screen. The company continue to enter and pass through the screen, moving back through the twentieth century, their costumes changing accordingly.

CHURCHILL: (*Voice-over.*) On this historic day, when India takes her place as a free and independent dominion in the British Commonwealth of Nations. I send you all my greetings and heartfelt wishes.

BBC: (*Voice-over.*) Here is a news flash: The German Radio has just announced that Hitler is dead. I'll repeat that. The German Radio has just announced that Hitler is dead.

CHAMBERLAIN: (*Voice-over.*) ...and no such undertaking has been received and consequently this country is at war with Germany.

The sound of war. Behind the screen, in silhouette, GANDHI crosses the stage.

GANDHI: (*Voice-over.*) There is an indefinable mysterious power that pervades everything. I feel it, though I do not see it. It is this unseen power which makes itself felt, and yet defies all proof.

HARDY enters. He walks into a spotlight in the centre of the stage as the screen rises, revealing only darkness behind.

HARVARD PROFESSOR: (*Voice-over.*) I am delighted to welcome, to the 1936 Harvard Conference on Arts and Science, Professor G H Hardy.

Applause. His back to the audience, HARDY begins to lecture into the darkness.

HARDY: I have set myself a task in these lectures which is genuinely difficult and which, if I were determined to begin by making every excuse for failure, I might represent as almost impossible. I have to form myself, as I have never really formed before, and to try to help you to form, some sort of reasoned estimate of the most romantic figure in the recent history of mathematics. A man who defies almost all of the canons by which we are accustomed to judge one another, and about whom all of us will probably agree in one judgement only, that he was a very great mathematician.

HARDY slowly dissolves offstage, as, in the darkness, we see three distant figures: RAMANUJAN, JANAKI and RAMANUJAN's MOTHER. As their voices echo in the space, RAMANUJAN begins to sink to the floor. He lies down as the women feed him, mop his brow.

RAMANUJAN: (*Voice-over.*) 20...19...18...17...16...15...14...13 ...12...11...10...

JANAKI: (*Voice-over.*) (*Speaking over the counting.*) Early on April 26, 1920, he lapsed into unconsciousness. For two hours I sat with him feeding him sips of diluted milk.

RAMANUJAN: (*Voice-over.*) ...9...8...7...6...5...4...3...2

Silence. Then a low intake of breath. JANAKI and RAMANUJAN's MOTHER throw their hands up in grief and dissolve offstage. In the distance upstage, a bed and a standing lamp, with a view of Cambridge behind. HARDY lies, as his sister GERTRUDE reads from a newspaper, her back to the audience.

GERTRUDE: 'W A Brown, caught Irani, bowled Amarnath – 11. A R Morris, hit the wicket, bowled Sarwate – 47. D G Bradman, not out – 179.' (*She looks down at HARDY.*) Harold? (*She reaches towards him. A moment.*) Oh Harold.

The lights fade as the sudden noise of a train approaches. The company move forward with chairs and form a line across the stage. SURITA sits on the far left, RUTH faces her. The screen flies in behind them and we see the view from a train as it speeds through the Indian countryside. AL watches.

PHONE: (*Voice-over.*) You have one saved message. Message left at 14.22, on January 23rd.

RUTH: (*Voice-over.*) Hello Al. I'm not coming home when I said I would. Don't worry. I'm on a train from Chennai to Kumbakonam and I'll call you when I get there. It's wonderful. Bye.

RUTH suddenly collapses forward. The other passengers rush towards her. There are shouts for help and water is passed along to her. In a rush of noise, the train disappears. Darkness.

...anigan went to
...d to speak in a
...age almost no one
...wood. But
...ps he did not

...on his own till he
...ying. That took
...12 months.

...nths in which to
...o love, to speak,
...am, to die.

I sit n...
the ac...
My fa...
diplo...
every...

father'...
broke...
He wa...
indepe...
made...

to Eng...
was a...
marrie...
east e...

throu...
centu...

4

The walls and whiteboard slide back into place and we return to the lecture hall. AL stands with his back to the audience, looks at the board. At his feet is the red suitcase and several boxes. Pause. An Indian CLEANER enters.

CLEANER: Excuse me? I have to clean this lecture hall.

AL: Sorry, go right ahead. I'm just collecting some stuff.

CLEANER empties the waste-paper bin and then moves to clean the whiteboard.

(*Moving to stop her.*) Could you leave that please?

CLEANER: Are you a lecturer?

AL: No. My wife's a lecturer. I'm collecting her stuff.

CLEANER: This lecture hall will be locked up in an hour.

A phone begins to ring.

AL: OK, I'll be out by then.

The CLEANER prepares to leave. Then she sees something on the board.

CLEANER: (*Correcting the equation.*) And that is infinity to the power of -1.

CLEANER exits. The phone continues to ring and AL searches in his pockets and boxes. Eventually he finds a phone and answers it.

AL: Cooper.

BARBARA: (*Voice-over.*) Mr Cooper? Hello there Mr Cooper! This is Ms Barbara Jones, calling from BT. How are you today?

AL: I'm fine thank you.

BARBARA: (*Voice-over.*) Wonderful! I understand you left a message with us. How can I help you today?

AL: (*Remembering.*) Oh... God...yes, I have a telephone number, but it's in someone else's name. I want to keep the telephone number and transfer it to my name.

BARBARA: (*Voice-over.*) Are you the account holder?

AL: No I'm not.

BARBARA: (*Voice-over.*) BT is obviously one of the best customer services available. What we can do for you Mr Cooper is we can offer you a brand new package, with a special ten per cent off for our existing customers. We can also send an engineer for you at your convenience. How does it sound for you Mr Cooper?

AL: That's very kind of you Barbara, but I don't want a brand new package. I want the same telephone number, I just want to change the name.

BARBARA: (*Voice-over.*) I tell you what we can do, Mr Cooper. If you'd like to give me your account details, I can input them into the system and we can see where we can go from there.

AL: OK.

BARBARA: (*Voice-over.*) If you'd like to start by giving me your telephone number.

AL: 0207 291 1729.

BARBARA: (*Voice-over.*) 0-2-0...

Pause.

AL: 0207 29...

BARBARA: (*Voice-over.*) 0-2-0-7

AL: 0207. That's a London number.

BARBARA: (*Voice-over.*) That is correct Mr Cooper, it is a London number.

AL: Where are you calling from?

BARBARA: (*Voice-over.*) I'm calling from BT Headquarters.

AL: Where's that? Bombay, Bangalore?

BARBARA: (*Voice-over.*) No, Mr Cooper, headquarters is in headquarters, OK? Wonderful! 020 7-

AL: 0207 291 1729.

BARBARA: (*Voice-over.*) 0-2-0-7 -2-9-1

AL: 0207 291…

BARBARA: (*Voice-over.*) …-2-9-1…

AL: You got the 291 part right?

BARBARA: (*Voice-over.*) Yes, I do, Mr Cooper.

AL: Well here come the next four – 1-7-2-9.

BARBARA: (*Voice-over.*) …1-7-2-9. Wonderful! Thank you very much Mr Cooper. We are through to the second stage of security. If I could take your mother's maiden name please?

AL: Masani.

Pause.

BARBARA: (*Voice-over.*) Oh dear, Mr Cooper, I'm afraid that is not the correct answer.

AL: Ah, right, you'll have my wife's mother's name, which is Van Oosteran.

BARBARA: (*Voice-over.*) Van…who?

AL: I'll spell it for you. You ready?

BARBARA: (*Voice-over.*) I'm always ready Mr Cooper!

AL: Here we go, V A N O…

BARBARA: (*Voice-over.*) V A N O… Oh! I'll just be one moment Mr Cooper, I'm going to put you on hold.

AL: Wait, wait!

BARBARA's voice disappears and is replaced by hold music. AL sits. He looks at the phone in his hand. The sound of a plane overhead. The lights dim. In the distance, upstage, in the half-light, stands RUTH – a memory.

RUTH: (*Voice-over.*) Al, it's Ruth, Ruth Minnen. You're
probably in Geneva by now… I just wanted to say thank
you for the other night. I had a really lovely time. I
probably didn't manage to assuage your worries about
infinity. But have a successful trip and do call any time,
next time you're in London. Bye. Oh! My number: 0207
291 1729. Bye.

*RUTH fades into darkness as, with the roar of another plane, the
screen flies out to reveal the departure lounge of Geneva Airport.
AL walks from the lecture hall into the airport and into his past.
He lifts the phone to his ear.*

(*Voice-over.*) Hello, this is Ruth Minnen's phone. Please
leave a message after the tone and I'll get back to you as
soon as I can. Thank you.

AL: Ruth, hi, it's Al, Al Cooper. I'm so psyched you called. I
want to ask you tonnes of questions about infinity. But I've
been obsessing about this because last night you said there
was some sort of special significance to your telephone
number and I wanted to see I could figure it out. So here
goes: it's not a palindrome 72911729 doesn't quite work.
The City of Baltimore where I was born was founded in
1729, but I doubt that would mean anything to YOU. I
was wondering, does it have anything to do with pi? The
irrational kind, not the edible kind. Because yesterday you
kept talking about that Indian mathematician guy who you
said had a special recipe for pi?

*ANINDA, also in the airport, steps forward. He, too, is on the
phone.*

ANINDA: 3142 extension, yes. (*Beat.*) Auntie, you're in
hospital, what's going on? No, you must stay in hospital.
Let the doctors look after you they know what they're
doing. I'm so sorry but I can't come and see you now
because I'm in CERN. CERN. Geneva. Switzerland. I'm
going to give a lecture. (*Beat.*) It doesn't matter what I'm
lecturing on. (*Beat.*) OK, if I tell you it's about Srinivasa
Ramanujan and string theory? (*Beat.*) No, I can't explain
string theory to you. (*Beat.*) I'm not patronising you it's

just rather a large subject. If I tell you that it is about
how everything in the universe is linked – will that satisfy
you? Yes, Auntie...like it says in the Upanishads all those
millennia ago, everything is connected to everything else.
But that doesn't matter now, what matters is that you get
well. You can ring me anytime. Well, I'll give it to you...
tell the nurse to get pen and paper, I'll wait...

*AL has moved back into the lecture hall and the present. The hold
music cuts out and...*

BARBARA: (*Voice-over.*) Mr Cooper, can I take your telephone
number again please?

AL: It's 0207...

BARBARA: (*Voice-over.*) 0...2...0...7...

ANINDA: (*Into phone.*) 00...41...for Switzerland, Auntie...

*And they are all speaking simultaneously. A chaotic jumble
of numbers. The sound of another passing aircraft and, as the
whiteboard flies back in, Geneva Airport disappears.*

AL: (*Still on phone.*) Hello Barbara? (*Pause.*) Hello? (*Silence.*)
Every fucking time.

He puts the phone down. Silence.

5

After a moment, AL picks up the suitcase and boxes and heads for the door. He pushes it. It's locked. He pushes again, nothing. Pause. He bangs on the door.

AL: Hello! Hello! Is anybody out there? Hello!

Silence. Then, with a click, the lights go out.

Oh shit!

AL stamps around in the darkness. Pause. Noticing the phone on the wall, he runs over and presses a button.

ANSWER PHONE: (*Voice-over.*) You are through to Uxbridge Campus of Brunel University. We are now closed. Office hours are 9 am until 5 pm. For enquiries outside these hours please call 01895 285000. That's 01895 285000. Thank you.

Beep.

AL: Hello, my name is Al Cooper, Ruth Minnen is my wife. I am stuck in Lecture Hall number 2. I'd be really grateful if someone could come down here and let me out. Thank you.

He hangs up the phone. Thinks. He pulls out his mobile and dials another number.

DAVID: (*Voice-over.*) Al, brilliant, I was going to call you…

AL: David, how are you?

DAVID: (*Voice-over.*) Great, they are getting very excited.

AL: David, I'm down here at Brunel picking up Ruth's stuff that came back from India…

DAVID: (*Voice-over.*) God, man, are you OK?

AL: Yeah, I'm fine, but something really stupid has happened. I've managed to get myself locked into a lecture hall; it's Lecture Hall Number 2. Now this is the last place on earth I want to be right now, Dave. So look, just get in a cab and come down here and get someone to let me out, I'll buy you a beer.

Pause.

DAVID: (*Voice-over.*) I can't.

AL: Why not?

DAVID: (*Voice-over.*) I'm in Los Angeles.

AL: Fuck.

AL leans on the desk and accidentally turns on the Overhead Projector. It casts a dim light over his face. Projected onto the high screen above the whiteboard is an image of AL's hand and, in the middle of the projector, a dead bee.

DAVID: (*Voice-over.*) I'm prepping for the meeting tomorrow. You said to be here early so we'd be set when you arrived for breakfast briefing.

AL: OK, OK, calm down. If I don't make it, you walk into that room, real calm and you tell them that their money is safe. We're going to close down the call centres; they're chump-change, we don't need them.

DAVID: (*Voice-over.*) They won't take that from me. They're hot for 'that Cooper guy'. You need to be here!

AL: You have to help me, David.

DAVID: (*Voice-over.*) What am I gonna do?

AL: I've done all I can, Dave. This is a new phone. I have no numbers in it. I've done all the calling I can do! Do NOT leave me in here all night!

DAVID: (*Voice-over.*) OK. Don't freak, Al. I'll sort it out. I'll call the police… I have got a mate in the fire service. No, no. (*Beat.*) Right, I still have the numbers of the guys in Ruth's department from when we had your stag do. I'll mobilise the geeks. So sit tight. We'll get you out. Just read a book or something.

AL: I don't HAVE any books. All I've got is a suitcase full of Ruth's fucking maths books.

DAVID: (*Voice-over.*) You've got to calm down, it might take an hour or two. The cavalry are coming! OK, I'm on it.

Pause. AL sees the bee in front of him.

AL: David, you know what? The weirdest thing, there's a dead bee in here. Dave? David?

But DAVID has gone. AL puts the phone away. A plane passes overhead, then silence. AL sits. He looks behind him and realises that the OHP is on. He dances his fingers over the screen and chuckles. Pause. He opens one of RUTH's boxes and looks through contents. He lifts out a piece of chalk and places in on the OHP. He lifts out a scarf, looks at it and sniffs it tenderly. Pause. He lifts out a pile of books, documents and a laptop computer. He lifts items from the top of the pile and places them on the OHP, where we see them projected on the high screen: RUTH's passport; A home pregnancy kit; A Rough Guide to India. He flicks through the pages. Stuffed inside is a photograph of AL and RUTH in bed together. AL quickly puts his hand over the photo. Pause. He turns the page and finds a period photograph of a young Indian man with a curious expression. AL closes the guidebook and puts it to one side. The next book in the pile is a thin green and white volume entitled A Mathematician's Apology. *AL places it on the OHP.*

G H Hardy. (*He opens the book and begins to read.*) 'It is a melancholy experience for a professional mathematician to find himself writing about mathematics…'

Through the screen, distant, HARDY at his desk in Cambridge.

HARDY: (*Voice-over.*) '…the function of a mathematician is to do something, to prove new theorems, to add to mathematics, and not to talk about what he and other mathematicians have done. The noblest ambition is that of leaving behind something of permanent value.'

AL: '…something of permanent value…'

HARDY fades into darkness as AL turns the pages. One page is marked in the margin, 'FOR AL'. He begins to read.

'A mathematician, like a painter or a poet is a maker of patterns…'

In the glass window of the door, RUTH's face appears. She enters and slowly moves across the stage towards AL. He continues to read, oblivious, as she stands and watches him.

RUTH: (*Voice-over.*) 'A mathematician, like a painter or a poet is a maker of patterns. If his patterns are more permanent than theirs it is because they are made of ideas. A painter makes patterns with shapes and colours, a poet with words. (*She places her hand next to his on the book.*) A mathematician on the other hand has nothing to work with but ideas, and so his patterns are likely to last longer, since ideas wear less with time than words.'

RUTH walks to the screen and places her hand up it. As she does so, numbers and formulae flow from her fingers. We glimpse HARDY, through the screen.

HARDY: (*Voice-over.*) 'The mathematician's patterns, like the painter's or the poet's, must be beautiful; the ideas, like the colours or the words, must fit together in a harmonious way. Beauty is the first test: there is no permanent place in the world for ugly mathematics.'

A rush of music and noise as RUTH passes through the screen and onto the streets of Chennai.

RUTH: (*Voice-over.*) Al, it's so beautiful here and hot. I don't understand why you've never come back. I wish you were with me. Madras is incredible. I'm standing in the library, at the window. I'm looking at the sea.

The Chennai Library appears. AL flicks through photographs of Chennai on the OHP, so that the images hover on the screen above the scene. The LIBRARIAN approaches RUTH. She carries an old notebook and several pages of documentation. She speaks in Tamil.

I'm sorry, I don't understand.

A passing STUDENT stops next to them.

STUDENT: Hello madam. She is just asking you to sign here, as this book is very fragile. She also says you must not take any photographs.

He moves on.

RUTH: Thank you. (*She signs the document, takes the notebook and sits at the desk.*) This is so exciting Al. I'm holding Ramanujan's notebooks in my hands. I'm feeling in the middle of things again. I turn page after page. I'm looking at the numbers. Whole sequences of them. They are scattered across the page like seeds 1…9…19…24. Everywhere the number 24. This is an example of what mathematicians call a magic number. Numbers that continually appear where we least expect them for reasons that no one can understand. And I don't understand, but they're beautiful…

AL: (*To himself.*) How can something you don't understand be beautiful?

RUTH: (*Turning to AL.*) Don't we call something 'beautiful' simply because it outpaces us? Imagine we're on a line. Ramanujan way ahead with Brahmagupta, who invented zero, and me, I'm far behind, if I look over my shoulder I see you.

RUTH steps out of the Library as the company begin a tihai. They form a line pointing diagonally towards AL, who stands and watches. RUTH is in the centre.

(*Voice-over.*) It may be very hard to define mathematical beauty but that is true of beauty of any kind. We may not know quite what we mean by a beautiful poem, but that does not prevent us from recognising one when we read it.

The company peel off one at a time and the line retreats away from AL. HARDY is left in the centre, at the desk, with the notebook.

HARDY: (*Voice-over.*) In these days of conflict, there must surely be something to be said for a study which did not begin with Pythagoras and will not end with Einstein, but is the oldest and youngest of all. The noblest ambition is that of leaving behind something of permanent value.

The screen flies back in and Chennai and HARDY disappear. AL opens RUTH's laptop. Types…

AL: R A M A N U J A N. Ramanujan.

6

ANINDA enters and walks to the lectern. Through the screen we see HARDY in Cambridge.

HARDY: (*Voice-over.*) 'Immortality' may be a silly word, but probably a mathematician has the best chance of it, whatever it may mean…

ANINDA appears on the screen in a small computer window.

ANINDA: …So said the mathematician GH Hardy in his *Mathematician's Apology* and forgive me if tonight I begin with the biographical before moving to the mathematical. But I believe that the permanence of his ideas must be put in context of the brevity of his life. Ultimately I will address myself to the vital contribution of his modular functions to the conformal symmetries required by string theory. But first let me say how honoured I am to be here with you tonight at the CERN Institute, home of the World Wide Web, so naturally we are being simultaneously podcasted…if that's the right verbiage.

AL carries the laptop to the floor and sits, watching the podcast.

The mathematician I will be speaking of is Srinivasa Ramanujan. Srinivasa Ramanujan was the strangest man in all mathematics, probably in the entire history of science. In his lecture about Ramanujan given at Harvard in 1936, GH Hardy, the mathematician who perhaps came to know him best, describes Ramanujan as 'the most romantic figure in the recent history of Mathematics'.

HARDY appears in silhouette behind the screen.

HARDY: (*Voice-over.*) A man who defies almost all of the canons by which we are accustomed to judge one another, and about whom all of us will probably agree in one judgement only, that he was a very great mathematician.

HARDY's silhouette slowly fades.

ANINDA: Hardy asked his audience to begin by trying to reconstruct the reaction of an ordinary professional mathematician who receives a letter from an unknown Hindu clerk.

Lights out!

(*The lights cut out as ANINDA moves to the OHP. He is illuminated by its light as he speaks.*) One morning, early in 1913, he found among the letters on his breakfast table a large untidy envelope, decorated with Indian stamps. (*ANINDA puts a letter on the OHP.*) When he opened it, he found line after line of symbols…strange theorems, theorems such as he had never seen before. (*The MUSICIAN plays the tabla. In the distance upstage, HARDY works at his desk.*)

He was, by this time, a world famous mathematician and world famous mathematicians, he had already discovered, are unusually exposed to cranks. He glanced at the letter, written in halting English by an unknown Indian, asking him to give an opinion on these mathematical discoveries. 1+2+3+4+5+ to infinity equals minus one twelfth. How could that possibly be? (*The MUSICIAN stops.*) He put the manuscript aside and went on with his day's routine. Since that routine did not vary throughout his life, it is possible to reconstruct it. First, he read *The Times* over his breakfast. (*ANINDA puts* The Times *on the OHP and centre-stage we see an aerial view of HARDY eating his breakfast.*) This happened in January, and if there were any Australian cricket scores, he would start with them, read with clarity and intense attention. Then, from about nine until one, unless he was giving a lecture, he worked at his own mathematics. (*ANINDA puts some sheets of mathematics on the OHP and we see an aerial view of HARDY working at his desk.*)

HARDY: (*Voice-over.*) Four hours creative work a day is about the limit for a mathematician…

ANINDA: …he would say. Then, lunch – a light meal in Hall. (*ANINDA rolls an apple across the OHP.*) After lunch he loped off for a game of real tennis in the university court.

(*HARDY plays tennis.*) At the back of his mind, the Indian manuscript nagged away. (*The MUSICIAN plays.*) When he returned to his rooms, he had another look at the script. He sent word to his colleague, Littlewood, that they must have a discussion after Hall. (*The tabla gets faster, as HARDY and other fellows eat at High Table. Around them, figures and theorems float in the air.*) Wild theorems, theorems such as he had never seen before nor imagined. A question was forming itself in his mind, 'Is a fraud of genius more probable than an unknown mathematician of genius?' Clearly, the answer was no. (*HARDY and LITTLEWOOD, in silhouette, studying the letter.*) By 9 o'clock or so they were in one of Hardy's rooms with the manuscript stretched out in front of them. It did not take them long. By midnight they knew, and knew for certain: (*The tabla stops suddenly.*) the writer of these manuscripts was a man of genius.

Silence, then music. Upstage, HARDY at his desk, reading. As RAMANUJAN speaks, a large photograph of his face appears projected over the whole stage, like a mirage. It is the photograph AL found earlier amongst RUTH's things. RUTH crosses the stage, behind. AL crosses front, carrying the laptop.

RAMANUJAN: (*Voice-over.*) Dear Sir, I beg to introduce myself to you as a clerk in the accounts department of the Port Trust Office at Madras on a salary of only £20 per annum. I am now about 23 years of age. I have had no University education but I have undergone the ordinary school course. (*AL's voice in the distance, counting.*) After leaving school I have been employing the spare time at my disposal to work at mathematics. I have not trodden through the conventional regular course which is followed in the university course, but I am striking out a new path for myself. I have made a special investigation of divergent series in general and the results I get are termed by the local mathematicians as 'startling'.

Slowly the photograph fades. ANINDA walks up to HARDY.

ANINDA: The following day, Hardy went into action. The man must be brought to England at once! His friend Bertrand Russell reported that he found Hardy 'in a state of wild excitement' because he believed he had discovered 'a second Newton'. Hardy began to draft a reply…

ANINDA exits and the music changes.

HARDY: (*Voice-over.*) Dear Mr Ramanujan, I was exceedingly interested by your letter and by the theorems which you state. Before I can judge properly the value of what you have done, it is essential that I should see proofs of some of your assertions. (*A portable blackboard crosses in front of HARDY and he vanishes. In his place, RAMANUJAN sits cross-legged with his back to us, working.*) I need not say that if what you say about your lack of training is to be taken literally, the fact that you should have rediscovered such interesting results is all to your credit.

The sound of an approaching train. The blackboard crosses and RAMANUJAN vanishes. RUTH and SURITA face each other on chairs in front of the board. Indian countryside rushes past.

RUTH: (*Voice-over.*) Hello Al, I'm not coming home when I said I would. Don't worry, I'm on a train from Chennai to Kumbakonam… I'm not coming home. I'm not coming home when I said I would.

A rush of noise and the train disappears.

AL: RUTH!

But AL is alone in the darkened lecture hall. He sits.

7

RUTH enters the lecture hall and turns on the light. AL stands.

AL: Ruth.

RUTH: Al, what on earth are you doing here?

AL: Waiting for you.

RUTH: You're supposed to be on a plane to Chicago.

AL: I had to ask you a question.

RUTH: I want you to go. I've got a lecture in 5 minutes.

AL: I'll watch.

RUTH: No. No watching.

AL: Why not?

RUTH: I'd feel exposed.

AL: I've seen you naked.

RUTH: Al, you can't say that now. People are going to be arriving any minute and I have to concentrate on convergent series.

AL: Do you want children?

RUTH: We're not together anymore!

AL: Do you want children?

RUTH: You said it was impossible, remember?

AL: I made a huge mistake. Do you want children?

RUTH: And I'm 40 years old.

AL: And I'm 41! Yesterday you said, 'the noblest ambition is that of leaving behind something of permanent value'.

RUTH: Actually, that was G H Hardy and he was talking about mathematics!

She picks up A Mathematician's Apology *from the desk and waves it at him.*

AL: And I'm talking about children.

RUTH: Mathematical creativity.

AL: PROcreativity.

RUTH: (*Pushing the book towards him.*) I want you to have it. Read it. He was a strange and extraordinary man.

AL: And you're a strange and extraordinary woman. I'm sorry.

He moves to her. They kiss. Suddenly RUTH breaks off and looks into the auditorium.

RUTH: Oh hello, yes, come in. (*Beat.*) That's fine, come in. (*She gestures to the entering students.*) Yes, sit in the middle.

AL: (*Waving at the class as they enter.*) Hi Marcus…you get the iPod? The Nano or the 80 gig? (*Quietly.*) Animal…

RUTH: Al, please sit down. (*He does so.*) Some series as they go off into infinity converge to a finite number.

AL: (*Quietly.*) Do you want children?

RUTH: (*Completely distracted but attempting to continue.*) That is to say, they get closer and closer to that number and only meet it in infinity.

AL: (*Quietly.*) Do you want children?

RUTH: A particularly beautiful convergent series of this nature is one plus a half plus a quarter plus an eighth plus a sixteenth and so on, which in infinity sums to two. (*She looks at AL.*) I hope that answers your question.

RUTH picks up the red suitcase and starts to walk towards the screen.

(*Voice-over.*) One plus a half plus a quarter plus an eighth plus a sixteenth plus one over thirty-two…

She disappears through the screen as a plane roars overhead. The screen flies out and reveals a row of chairs, one behind the other – a plane. AL takes his seat in the middle.

CAPTAIN: (*Voice-over.*) Ladies and gentlemen, the 'Fasten Your Seatbelt' sign is now illuminated. We are experiencing a little turbulence at the moment, which as you may know is simply due to convergent weather systems resulting in pockets of variable air pressure. Nothing to worry about. Apologies again for the delay...

RUTH: (*Voice-over.*) Hello Al, you must be somewhere over the Atlantic by now. I can't come home when I said I would. I'm on a train from Chennai to Kumbakonam and it's wonderful. I miss you, bye...

The plane disintegrates, leaving RUTH, sat on her suitcase upstage. Music.

HARDY: (*Voice-over.*) Dear Mr Ramanujan, I was exceedingly interested by your letter and by the theorems which you state...

The portable blackboard moves quickly across in front of RUTH. She disappears and in her place is RAMANUJAN, working, in the same position as before.

RAMANUJAN: (*Voice-over.*) Dear Sir, I am much gratified on perusing your letter. I have found in you a friend who views my labours sympathetically. What I want at this stage is for eminent professors like you to recognise that there is some worth in me...

The board passes again, RAMANUJAN disappears and HARDY is revealed, sat at his desk.

HARDY: (*Voice-over.*) It has been suggested to me that your unwillingness to give proofs may be due to apprehensions as to the use I might make of your results...

The board passes, HARDY disappears and RAMANUJAN sits facing outwards. His MOTHER enters, carrying food for him.

RAMANUJAN: (*Voice-over.*) ...I am a little pained to see what you have written. I am not in the least apprehensive of my method being utilised by others. On the contrary, my method has been in my possession for the last eight years and I have not found anyone to appreciate the method...

The board rotates and reveals HARDY. It moves between him and RAMANUJAN, one on either side, and they both begin to write upon it.

HARDY: (*Voice-over.*) I am delighted to extend a formal invitation, on behalf of the college, for you to come to Cambridge and continue your work. This would of course carry with it some form of scholarship, assistance with accommodation and so on. All of which can be discussed in due course...

RAMANUJAN and HARDY advance downstage, the blackboard circling between them.

RAMANUJAN: (*Voice-over.*) Dear Sir, I am delighted that not only yourself but also other mathematicians at the very fountainhead of mathematical knowledge are interesting themselves in my humble work, but I regret that I will not be able to come to England. My superior officer, a very orthodox Brahmin, of the same caste as myself, told me that I could not go to England and the matter has been dropped.

The board sweeps in front of RAMANUJAN and he disappears. HARDY exits. The noise of a train.

8

The screen flies in and in front of it the Chennai train appears. The countryside flies past.

RUTH: (*Voice-over.*) Hello Al, I'm not coming home when I said I would…hello Al, don't worry… I'm not coming home when I said I would…

SURITA and RUTH face each other. SURITA is talking loudly over the noise of the train.

SURITA: No, this is my first time.

RUTH: What?

SURITA: This is my first time…in India.

RUTH: Your first time? How have you found it?

SURITA: Overwhelming!

RUTH: And hot.

SURITA: Yeah, steaming!

RUTH: I'm Ruth.

SURITA: Surita Bhogaita. You been before?

RUTH: No, this is my first time too. So are you on holiday?

SURITA: Yes, My Auntie is getting married in Gujarat.

RUTH: The north, that's miles away.

SURITA: I know… I think she's trying to set me up with some nice Brahmin boy!

RUTH: You're a Brahmin?

SURITA: Yes.

RUTH: You never wanted to come before?

SURITA: Well I was born in England, and my parents were born in Uganda. And my great grandparents left India in 1869 so India for me is 150 years away.

RUTH: So is it what you expected it to be?

SURITA: No! I feel so disconnected. I'm an outsider.

RUTH: Can I ask you something? Brahmin men, they wear a string across their body...

Her voice tails off and she holds her head.

SURITA: Are you alright?

RUTH: Yes...what does the string signify?

SURITA: It's three threads that are intertwined and represent thought, word and deed. Did you go to the temples in Chennai?

RUTH: No, I went to the library.

SURITA: You were in the library on holiday?

RUTH: Yes, it was amazing. Oh, excuse me. (*She dials on her phone.*) Hello Al, I'm not coming home when I said I would...

Train noise, the screen rises and the passengers turn their chairs upstage into the darkness, except SURITA who remains looking out. ANINDA steps out of the middle of the train.

ANINDA: Like me, Ramanujan was a Brahmin. For a Brahmin, such as he was, unusually strict about his religious observances with a mother who was even stricter, crossing the water from native lands was strictly forbidden. To become an exile was to become an outcast.

It begins to rain. HARDY appears with an umbrella.

HARDY: (*Voice-over.*) Dear Neville, I'm writing in a hurry to catch the mail and warn you to be a little careful. I've been in correspondence with the Indian Office again. In order that Ramanujan should come – and of that I'm as anxious as ever – a great deal of subtlety will be required... (*HARDY hands a letter to ANINDA and closes his umbrella.*) Dear Mr Ramanujan, try to make the acquaintance of Mr E H Neville, who is in Madras lecturing. He comes from my college and you may find his advice as to reading and study invaluable.

RAMANUJAN, JANAKI and RAMANUJAN's MOTHER enter and sit. RAMANUJAN works and the women feed him.

RAMANUJAN: (*Voice-over.*) I went to Mr Neville of your college who very kindly spoke to me and cleared my doubts that I need not care for my expenses, that my English will do, that I am not asked to go to England to appear for any examination and that I can remain a vegetarian there.

ANINDA: What made him change his mind? Was it a dream in a temple or was it his mother's vision of him in Cambridge? We may never know, but I believe it was the mathematics that lured him.

ANINDA hands him HARDY's letter. RAMANUJAN reads.

RAMANUJAN: (*Voice-over.*) He also pointed out to me the benefits I derive from coming into contact with modern mathematicians and modern ways of thinking. So I am now booked on the SS Nevasa, which leaves Madras on the 17th. Yours, very sincerely, S. Ramanujan.

Music. JANAKI and RAMANUJAN's MOTHER exit as RAMANUJAN begins to stand, turning his body as he does and pouring salt from his workboard.

ANINDA: At about ten o'clock on the morning of March 17, 1914, the SS Nevasa slipped slowly away from the dock.

The sounds of a ship and of the sea. RAMANUJAN is joined by the rest of the company who stand in a line, looking out, SURITA on the left. She listens.

YOUNG WOMAN: (*Voice-over.*) I remember standing on the rail of the boat as it pulled away from India. And my parents were both crying and crying and India was getting smaller and smaller and all the lights were getting dimmer and dimmer. And they were crying because they knew they'd never see her again.

RAMANUJAN moves far upstage and begins to dress.

RAMANUJAN: (*Voice-over.*) Madras is at the latitude of 13 degrees north, a prime number. The ship travels south to the latitude of 7 degrees north, also a prime number.

ANINDA: All his life he wore the dhoti, his hair in the kudumi and always the very important Brahmin string, whose three threads symbolise body, mind and soul inextricably entwined.

RAMANUJAN: (*Voice-over.*) For the first three days I was very uncomfortable and took very little food but after that I have been alright. The sea is very smooth and there is no fear of seasickness. I do not know whether I have to go to Cambridge directly or stay at London and then go. I shall write to you after I reach England and everything is definitely settled. I am, yours very sincerely, S Ramanujan.

The sound of an aircraft and the plane forms again centrestage, AL sat at the head. ANINDA slowly moves a bed, covered in a white blanket, downstage past the chairs.

CAPTAIN: (*Voice-over.*) Ladies and gentlemen, we are now cruising at an altitude of 33,000 feet on a latitude of 67 degrees north. We are currently passing over Greenland. If you look out of your windows you'll see the polar ice caps down below. (*The passengers look out at the passing bed.*) Quite magnificent. Do enjoy the rest of your flight, ladies and gentlemen. I'm afraid the weather they have lined up for us in London is cold, grey and wet.

The plane dissolves. A map projected upstage shows the journey from India to London.

INDIAN VOICE: (*Voice-over.*) Though one sits in meditation in a particular place, the self within can exercise his influence far away. Though still, he moves everything everywhere.

RAMANUJAN: (*Voice-over.*) The ship enters the Atlantic Ocean and heads due north to a latitude of 47 degrees then turns right into the English Channel before arriving in London at a latitude of 53 degrees – another prime number.

HARDY stands, waiting, under his umbrella.

ANINDA: On 14th of April, 112 days before the start of the First World War, Ramanujan finally arrived in Cambridge.

RAMANUJAN emerges in the distance. He wears a suit. Behind him, Trinity College comes into focus.

HARDY: Mr Ramanujan!

He moves towards him.

ANINDA: Now the dhoti, the kudumi and the Brahmin string were to be discarded for suit and shoes and cropped hair.

RAMANUJAN and HARDY meet centrestage. The sound of lift-doors opening. They turn away and AL is revealed behind them.

9

AL steps forward into his hotel room. The bed is unmade.

TELEVISION INTRODUCTION: (*Voice-over.*) Welcome to the
Ramada Inn Heathrow.

AL picks the phone from the wall.

AL: Good evening. I'm in room 1024. My bed is unmade and
it's freezing in here. Can I change rooms? No, I don't want
anything on the 13th floor. Well, could you send someone
up to fix this please? OK, thanks.

*He replaces the phone and points a remote at the corner of the
stage. The TV channel changes. In the distance, upstage, Trinity
College emerges from the darkness.*

TELEVISION INTRODUCTION: (*Voice-over.*) While you're here
why not take a day trip to one of the picturesque towns
in the region? Windsor, Bath, Oxford and Cambridge are
all within easy reach. You can book a day trip with our
dedicated travel adviser; just press the red button on your
remote control for further information.

*AL sits on the bed. He changes channels with the remote. Choral
music and different images of Trinity in the distance. RAMANUJAN
stands in the centre. Figures in gowns emerge from the darkness
and start placing books around the stage.*

CAMBRIDGE TOUR GUIDE: (*Voice-over.*) Cambridge lies
approximately 50 miles north-northeast of London. In 1209
a group of students from Oxford established a University
there... Trinity College was founded by Henry VIII in 1546
and is the largest of the Cambridge and Oxford colleges...

*The TV sound fades. RAMANUJAN sits in the centre of the books.
He slips off his shoes and puts on slippers. Awkwardly he shuffles
off into the darkness.*

TRINITY ALUMNI: (*Voice-over.*) We only knew that his name
was Ramanujan and even this was pronounced wrongly. We
didn't often see him but when we did, we noticed him – his

squat, solitary figure as he waddled across Great Court, his feet in slippers, as he was unable to wear shoes.

AL changes channels with the remote. The sound of pornography from the TV – music and groaning. AL grins, sighs and points the remote. Nothing happens. He looks at the remote and tries again. Nothing – he can't turn it off. He starts jabbing at the remote and the sound starts to get louder and louder. Enter SURITA. She wears an apron and carries a fruit-basket. A moment as she takes in the scene.

SURITA: Excuse me!

AL can't hear her above the increasing noise of the pornography.

Excuse me!

SURITA approaches from behind him and touches his shoulder. AL jumps. He freezes.

I'll come back later!

AL: No, no! Help me. Help me, I can't turn it off.

AL hands SURITA the remote control and she switches the TV off. Slight pause.

SURITA: I'll come back later.

AL: It just came on.

SURITA: It's alright.

AL: It just came on!

SURITA: I'll come back later.

AL: I'm happily married with six kids!

SURITA: And I will come back later!

AL: I don't do porn. I find it emotionally degrading.

Pause.

SURITA: Shall I make your bed?

AL: OK. (*Pause. SURITA starts to make up the bed.*) That was a lie. I don't really have six kids. But I did just get married. I work in the futures market and in the futures market if you say something is going to happen it exponentially increases the chances of it happening.

SURITA: Good luck with that. (*Indicating the fruit.*) Compliments of the hotel, sorry the room wasn't ready for you.

AL: My mom used to do what you do.

SURITA: Excuse me?

AL: She used to be a chambermaid at the Ramada.

SURITA: This isn't what I do. I do this to pay off my student loan.

AL: (*Looking at her name badge.*) Where are you from… Surita?

SURITA: London… Ealing.

AL: Before that?

SURITA: Greenford. Where are you from?

AL: Los Angeles, California.

SURITA: Yeah, before that?

AL: New York, New York.

SURITA: (*Grinning.*) And before that?

AL: (*Grinning back.*) Baltimore, Maryland. (*Pause.*) But my parents were born in Bombay.

SURITA: Mumbai.

AL: Bombay. They got married and they moved to New Jersey and then we all moved to Baltimore just before I was born. So, I'm an American.

SURITA: I'm British.

AL: Before that?

The MUSICIAN sings softly.

SURITA: My parents were born in Uganda. They left in 1972: they were exiled. My grandparents originated from Gujurat. So, I'm Gujarati.

Behind her, in a diagonal line, appear SURITA's GRANDPARENTS. A moment, before RAMANUJAN passes down the line and swaps positions with AL and SURITA. He moves to the downstage bed, they move to the identical upstage bed. He sits. Picks an apple from the fruit basket.

RAMANUJAN: (*Voice-over.*) My dear Krishna Rao, this week has been cold with some snowfall. Everything here is strange and I was not well till the beginning of this term owing to the poor weather and the lack of proper food. At the moment the only fruit I can find is apples, so I would be grateful for supplies from home. I was silent so long as I had nothing to write to you but Professor Hardy and I will be presenting an important paper on our work on partitions and our development of the partition function.

SURITA is about to leave.

SURITA: So if there's anything else we can do, please let us know. (*She turns back.*) Oh and by the way, 'Shaven Babes' is on Channel 5: I've heard it's much better.

AL: (*Unthinking.*) Thank you. (*He realises what she just said.*) Hey!

But SURITA has gone. AL puts his head in his hands. He is alone.

(*Shouting.*) Ruth! The only place I feel at home anymore is with you. Call me.

10

RUTH enters through the door. Upstage HARDY sits at his desk in Cambridge.

RUTH: Call me, Al. (*Pause.*) I don't know what time zone you're on at the moment. I really need to speak to you in the next half hour. I'm at home. Bye.

She picks up a box from the desk and leaves again the way she came.

HARDY: The partition of a number is an expression of the number as a sum of positive integers.

ANINDA: When we think of partitioning a number, what we are talking about is splitting that number up into a sum of other numbers. For example ten could be six plus four. Now let us take one. The number of ways of partitioning one is one. So the number of partitions of one is one. Two may be written as two or one plus one. So the number of partitions of two is two.

RAMANUJAN moves to the desk and works with HARDY, passing papers between them. The sound of a toilet flushing. RUTH comes back through the door. She holds something in her hand. She stands to one side of ANINDA. AL stands on the other side. He is lost in memory.

Three may be written as three or as two plus one or as one plus one plus one. So the number of partitions of three is three. (*RUTH sits on the downstage bed. She slips off her shoes and arranges them on the floor. As ANINDA speaks, she makes the partitions with her feet and shoes.*) Four may be written as four, as three plus one, as two plus two, as two plus one plus one or as one plus one plus one plus one. So the number of partitions of four is five.

Suddenly, RUTH gasps at the object in her hand. She tries to make a phone call, but the line is engaged. Throughout the scene she continues to try to get through. ANINDA walks back upstage to where HARDY and RAMANUJAN work.

ANINDA: Five may be written as five, four plus one, three plus two, three plus one plus one, two plus two plus one, two plus one plus one plus one, or as one plus one plus one plus one plus one, so the number of partitions of five is seven. As we consider even slightly larger numbers the number of partitions increases rapidly. So the number of partitions of 7 is 15, the number of partitions of 10 is 42 and the number of partitions of 50 is 204,226.

HARDY: (*He writes on the portable blackboard.*) The partitioning of integers appears remarkably simple, but arriving at a general function that gives us precisely the number of partitions for any number is extremely complicated.

ANINDA: So complicated that 20th-century mathematicians had given up on it.

RAMANUJAN takes over writing on the board.

HARDY: For a large number such as 200 a formula yielding a result within several millions of the correct number of partitions would be an astonishing achievement. You would probably be pleased with an error in the order of billions but you might hope for millions.

RAMANUJAN: (*Voice-over.*) The answer for the partitions of two hundred is 3 million million, 972 thousand million, 999 million, 29 thousand, 3 hundred and 88. Our formula came within .004 of the correct integer.

As he finishes writing the formula, JANAKI and his MOTHER appear next to him. They pass through the blackboard.

HARDY: All beautiful theorems require a very high degree of economy, unexpectedness and inevitability. In his work on the partition function, Ramanujan beautifully intertwined all three.

RUTH is still dialling. This time, she gets through. At the desk, AL lifts his phone and speaks into it.

AL: Hello?

The mathematics from the small blackboard slowly grows until it fills the entire stage.

RUTH: Al, I've found you.

AL: Hello?

RUTH: What's one plus one?

A large white zero appears on RUTH's stomach.

AL: Hello?

RUTH: No Al! It's not two…it's three! Al, I'm pregnant! I'm pregnant!

RUTH collapses onto the bed in delight. In the present, AL is alone in the darkness.

AL: Hello?

BARBARA: (*Voice-over.*) Congratulations Mr Cooper! This is Barbara Jones calling from BT. How are you today?

AL: I'm fine. Why are you congratulating me?

BARBARA: (*Voice-over.*) I'm calling to say congratulations because we have successfully completed your application for a new telephone number. We can also offer you a brand new handset, just come on the market, available with free bluetooth. How do you feel?

AL: I don't want a new telephone number. I just want the same number and a different name.

BARBARA: (*Voice-over.*) But we have successfully completed your application. Obviously there has been some misunderstanding.

AL: (*Losing his temper.*) What do you mean misunderstanding? You people just try to sell people shit. That's all you're fucking about. I told you 0207 291 1729. 1729! That number means a lot to me!

BARBARA: (*Voice-over.*) (*Shaken by his outburst.*) There is no need for your distress. I'll go back to the system and see if I can rectify the situation for you. My greatest apologises on behalf of BT.

Pause.

AL: I'm sorry. I lost my temper.

BARBARA: (*Voice-over.*) (*Quieter.*) It is OK Mr Cooper. I understand it's a very important number for you. (*Beat.*) You are waking up on the wrong bedside today, eh Mr Cooper?

AL: What time is it?

BARBARA: (*Voice-over.*) It's about eight o'clock in the morning.

AL: It's about two thirty in the morning here, so obviously you're not in the UK.

BARBARA: (*Voice-over.*) (*Laughing.*) Ah…you got me there, Mr Cooper! Now you are being in a very cheeky cheeky mood!

AL: Where are you, Bombay? Bangalore?

BARBARA: (*Voice-over.*) Yes, I'm calling from Bangalore.

AL: (*Smiles.*) I knew it. What's the weather like in Bangalore?

BARBARA: (*Voice-over.*) The weather in Bangalore is beautiful as always. How is the weather in the UK?

AL: I don't know…because I'm locked in a lecture hall.

BARBARA: (*Voice-over.*) That is very unfortunate for you, Mr Cooper.

AL: Knowing this country it's probably peeing down outside.

BARBARA: (*Voice-over.*) But how would you know…you're locked in a lecture room.

Pause. AL smiles.

AL: You have a very nice voice.

BARBARA: (*Voice-over.*) Thank you. My husband does seem to think so. Are you married Mr Cooper?

Pause.

AL: It's really nice speaking to you, Barbara.

BARBARA: (*Voice-over.*) It's always lovely speaking to you, Mr Cooper.

AL: (*Grin.*) We've only spoken twice.

BARBARA: (*Voice-over.*) Yes, but each time has been a wonderful experience. Mr Cooper, I'll go back to the system and hopefully next time I will give you some very good news.

AL: Thank you. And Barbara? I expect to be here for a while, so…call me any time.

BARBARA: (*Voice-over.*) I shall call you anytime, Mr Cooper. Bye!

AL: Goodbye.

AL puts his phone down. A moment.

11

RAMANUJAN's MOTHER enters far upstage. She sings. She holds a small puppet boy by the hand and crosses the space. RUTH sits up in bed.

RUTH: When Ramanujan was a little boy he was asking deep mathematical questions. His maths teacher was explaining to the young class that any number or quantity divided by itself is equal to one. (*AL walks to the bed and kneels.*) So if you have three oranges and divide them between three boys each boy will get one, or if you have 40 fishes and 40 boys each boy will get one, and Ramanujan put up his hand and said 'are you saying any number divided by itself will equal one?' and the teacher said 'yes, even if you have 1,000 fishes and 1,000 boys each one will get one'. And Ramanujan said, 'so if you have no fishes and no boys will each one still get one?' Thereby touching on one of the most fundamental problems about zero – is zero divided by zero equal to one, or is zero divided by zero zero, or is zero divided by zero infinity? And the only certain thing about this problem is that it is uncertain. The answer depends upon the way you look at it.

Music. RAMANUJAN's MOTHER lifts up the puppet and carries him off into the darkness.

AL: Why on earth did you fall in love with me? (*Beat.*) Don't say it's because I look like Ramanujan.

RUTH: You give me hope for the future. Why did you fall in love with me?

AL: Because you're incomprehensible! Because you wouldn't kiss me on our first date...because you're the sweetest thing on earth...because you take away my panic...because you're a genius...because you have a secret world in there that I don't have access to. But I am trying. I'm trying so hard. (*Beat.*) I was thinking of this one on the plane, I think I like this one: one plus a half, plus a quarter, plus an eighth and then it eventually gets to two.

RUTH: Only in infinity.

AL: Yeah, but it gets to two.

RUTH: In infinity. It's a convergent infinite series. It's very beautiful.

AL: But…it gets there?

RUTH: No. It gets closer and closer and closer and closer and closer but never actually gets there.

Pause.

AL: Well then, I don't like it. Move over. (*He tries to lie down.*) It's a bit crowded in here!

RUTH: Three in a bed.

AL: Three in a bed. One… (*He kisses her face.*) …two… (*He kisses her stomach.*) …three. (*He climbs in next to her. A moment, then…*) What was Ramanujan famous for?

RUTH: His maths.

AL: What did his maths do?

RUTH: It didn't do anything. It's just maths.

AL: It's got to do something. What's his legacy?

RUTH: (*Suddenly grumpy.*) Al, I don't want to talk.

She pushes him out of bed. He lands hard on the floor. Looks at her.

AL: Jeez! Ow. (*Beat.*) What's the difference between a pregnant woman and a terrorist?

RUTH: I don't know.

AL: You can negotiate with a terrorist. (*He picks up the laptop.*) Why do you still have this ancient piece of crap?

He turns it on. Presses a button. RUTH sleeps. AL watches something.

REPORTER: (*Voice-over.*) Researchers say the bees are over-worked and are dying in the fields, perhaps becoming exhausted or simply disorientated and eventually falling victim to the cold. They are calling this phenomenon 'colony collapse disorder' and they say it may be due to the massive corporatisation of the American Honeybee. And experts say, 'No Bees, No Planet'.

Music. Enter RAMANUJAN's MOTHER and JANAKI, distant. They speak in Tamil.

RUTH: (*Looking up from the bed.*) Ramanujan's legacy is his work.

ANINDA: (*Stepping between the Indian women.*) Which consists of 4000 formulas on 400 pages filling three volumes of notes, all densely packed with theorems of incredible power.

RUTH gets out of the bed, where RAMANUJAN is now revealed, sleeping. She looks at him.

RUTH: He seemed to have functioned in a way unlike anyone else we know of. He had such a feel for things that…

RUTH / ANINDA: (*Together.*) …they just flowed out of his brain.

JANAKI and RAMANUJAN's MOTHER wake him, feed him. Behind them, we glimpse the Cauvery River.

JANAKI: (*Voice-over.*) At home in Madras he would ask his mother or myself to wake him after midnight so that the current of his thoughts might not be broken.

ANINDA: Perhaps he didn't see them in a way that was translatable. Hardy said:

HARDY appears at his desk. He moves forward with RUTH and ANINDA.

HARDY: It was like watching somebody at a feast, a feast you haven't been invited to. All his results, new or old, right or wrong, had been arrived at by a process of mingled argument, intuition and induction, of which he was entirely unable to give any coherent account.

RAMANUJAN stands, leaves his family without a word and walks towards HARDY. He puts on a large overcoat.

RAMANUJAN: (*Voice-over.*) My only problem is food. In this place there is no provision for vegetarians. I long for curd or vendakkai, anything from home. (*JANAKI walks past RAMANUJAN carrying food. They are in different worlds and cannot see each other. She exits.*) I have no choice but to cook for myself with whatever I can find: milk, carrots, rice, sometimes lemons. This term I have already published four pamphlets and one long paper.

HARDY: Working with him, it was impossible to ask such a man to submit to systematic instruction; he had his own way.

HARDY and RAMANUJAN work together at the desk. Behind them, RAMANUJAN's MOTHER begins to move, echoing their prosaic gestures with Bharatanatyam dance.

(*Voice-over.*) It seemed ridiculous to worry him about how he had found this or that known theorem, when he was showing me half a dozen new ones every day.

RAMANUJAN: (*Voice-over.*) I find myself working for 30 hours non-stop. And then I sleep for 20.

HARDY: You infer that pi of x remains finite as x approaches zero. There is no theorem I know of which warrants such a conclusion. How did you...? (*RAMANUJAN simply continues to work.*) Goodnight.

HARDY steps back and RAMANUJAN works alone.

RAMANUJAN: (*Voice-over.*) Immediately I heard the problem it was obvious that the solution should be a continued fraction: I then thought, 'which continued fraction?' and the answer came into my mind.

The company begin the 'Conference' tihai.

HARDY: To try to learn mathematics from the beginning once more would have been absurd for him. I was afraid that, if I insisted unduly on matters which he found irksome, I might destroy his confidence or break the spell of his inspiration.

The tihai continues as RAMANUJAN pushes papers off the desk. ANINDA, RUTH and the rest of the company spread the papers out on the floor around him, forming an enormous circle, with RAMANUJAN at the centre. HARDY circles the stage on a bike. Projected everywhere, numbers fall like snow.

RAMANUJAN: (*Voice-over.*) Ideas, like all human needs – food, sleep, warmth – require a search, a going elsewhere. In our imaginations we leave the immediately present, the centre of the circle, and when we do so we begin to count.

The tihai climaxes and HARDY exits on his bike. Upstage in the distance, Trinity College appears on the blackboard in the snow.

ANINDA: When we move away from zero we notice that counting, regularity, symmetry…also exist in nature. This is startling because it means that our imaginations are all working within another, infinitely larger imagination.

RAMANUJAN disappears through the blackboard. His silhouette appears in the snow. He catches snowflakes.

RAMANUJAN: (*Voice-over.*) There is nobody here except Professor Hardy as examinations are all over and all have gone outside.

AL sits up.

AL: One plus a half is one and a half plus a quarter is one and three quarters, plus an eighth is one and seven eighths, plus a sixteenth is one and fifteen sixteenths plus a thirty tooth…

RUTH sits up in bed.

RUTH: No, you say one over thirty-two. I'm going to the toilet.

RUTH exits. AL continues counting.

AL: …is one and thirty one thirty-tooths. Plus a sixty-fourth is one and sixty-three sixty-fourths.

RUTH: Al?

AL: Plus one one hundred and twenty-eighths is one……

RUTH enters. There's something on her fingers.

RUTH: Al?

AL: Yes?…is one and one hundred and twenty-seven one hundred and twenty-eighths…

RUTH: Al, there's a little bit of blood.

AL: What does that mean?

RUTH: I don't know. I'm bleeding.

AL: Oh shit. What shall we do?

RUTH: I don't know.

AL: Should I call the doctor?

RUTH: Yes.

AL: Let's just go. I'll get the car.

He starts to leave.

RUTH: No! Al don't leave me. I'm bleeding, I'm bleeding… Al! (*Howls.*) OH NO…

A sudden burst of music as they grab each other. Slowly, RUTH rolls over bed. AL rolls after her.

12

HARDY: (*Voice-over.*) We have still one more question to consider. We have still to ask whether mathematics does harm. (*Pause.*) It would be paradoxical to suggest that mathematics of any sort does much harm in times of peace, so that we are driven to the consideration of the effects of mathematics on war.

In the distance upstage, a line of figures, including HARDY and two First World War NURSES. RUTH stands.

JACKSON: (*Voice-over.*) At Cambridge we are in darkness. It is a new Cambridge, with 1,700 men in statu pupillari instead of 3,600. Medical Captains in khaki dine in hall by candlelight. On August 14th an ambulance with a great red cross on its side bore the first wounded patient to Trinity and what is now officially the First Eastern General Hospital. Sadly, yesterday that patient died from his wounds.

RUTH kicks over one of the books. The sounds of far-off gunfire as the company begin to walk amongst the books. AL stands.

RUTH: In biology, decomposition is the reduction of a formerly living organism into simpler forms of matter, such as phosphate of calcium or calcium carbonate – chalk. In mathematics, decomposition operates similarly by the reduction of a number to the multiplicative products of its prime. (*Pause. AL approaches RUTH and reaches a hand towards her.*) I'm sorry, I'll have to continue this later.

RUTH walks away and joins the rest of the company. AL remains standing, alone. ANINDA moves forward. Music.

ANINDA: 24, for example, can be reduced to 2 x 2 x 2 x 3 or 2 cubed x 3. So prime numbers are the bones of mathematics. Everything is built on them.

HARDY: (*Voice-over.*) I believe that pure mathematics has no effects on war; the real mathematician has his conscience clear.

RUTH: (*Voice-over.*) What is 2 cubed?

Music and gunfire and the company knock over books.

HARDY: (*Voice-over.*) The trivial mathematics on the other hand has many applications in war.

RUTH: (*Voice-over.*) What is 2 cubed times 3 squared?

Music and gunfire and the company knock over books.

HARDY: (*Voice-over.*) The gunnery experts and aeroplane designers could not do their work without it.

AL begins to collect up the papers.

RUTH: (*Voice-over.*) What is 2 cubed times 3 squared times 5?

Music and gunfire and the company knock over books.

HARDY: (*Voice-over.*) Mathematics facilitates modern, scientific, total war.

RUTH: (*Voice-over.*) What is 2 cubed times 3 squared times 5 times 7?

Music and gunfire and the company knock over books.

RAMAUNUJAN: (*Voice-over.*) 11 September, 1914, Trinity College. Ramanujan makes his countless prostrations to his mother and writes. You need not send any provisions. There is no war in this country. War is going on only in the neighbouring country. That is to say, war is waged in a country that is as far as Rangoon is away from Madras. No war like this has raged before.

RUTH: (*Voice-over.*) What is 2 cubed times 3 squared times 5 times 7 times 11 times 13?

Music and gunfire and the company knock over books.

RAMANUJAN: (*Voice-over.*) The present war afflicts crores of people. It is not only one or two crores. Germans set fire to many a city, slaughter and throw away all the people. The small country of Belgium is almost destroyed.

RUTH: (*Voice-over.*) 2 cubed times 3 squared times 5 times 7 times 11 times 13 times 97 equals 34,954,920.

Music and gunfire and the company knock over books.

HARDY: (*Voice-over.*) It can be maintained that modern warfare is less horrible than the warfare of pre-scientific times; that bombs are more merciful than bayonets and that anything is better than the concentration of savagery on one particular class; and that, in short, the sooner war becomes all out the better.

AL cradles the bundle of papers in his arms. It resembles a baby.

RUTH: (*Voice-over.*) 34,954,920. The number of dead, wounded and missing in the First World War.

A baby cries.

HARDY: (*Voice-over.*) When the world is mad, a mathematician may find in mathematics an incomparable anodyne.

AL pushes the papers into a wastepaper bin under the desk.

ANINDA: (*Voice-over.*) Had it not been for the Ramanujan collaboration, the First World War would have been darker for Hardy than it was. But it was dark enough.

For a moment HARDY is alone as the company move into the darkness.

HARDY: (*Voice-over.*) When the world is mad, a mathematician may find in mathematics an incomparable anodyne.

RUTH appears behind the desk and OHP. The lights of the lecture hall rise upon her. AL sits on the bed.

RUTH: I would like this evening to talk to you about nothing… zero…a particularly interesting number.

ANINDA: The Greeks had no zero, nor the Romans and neither did Europe until it arrived from India, over 800 years ago.

RUTH: I'd like to look at some of its mysterious properties by considering it rationally, that is to say by putting it into a fraction. (*She writes 1/ 0 on the OHP.*) What would happen if you put 0 on the bottom of a fraction? Let us imagine any fraction with 0 as the denominator. Let's take our most simple reciprocal function, y equals one over x. (*She writes the formula on the OHP and starts to draw a graph.*) I put this horizontal as my x axis and this vertical as my y axis, then I can plot a set of points where y equals one over x.

Music. Ramanujan stands in his pyjamas.

RAMANUJAN: (*Voice-over.*) I have made a serious mathematical assessment of my own horoscope and there is no doubt about it: I will die before I reach the age of thirty-five.

ANINDA: We are now approaching the difficult and tragic part of Ramanujan's career and we must try to understand what we can of the atmosphere surrounding him.

Slowly, the two NURSES help RAMANUJAN into a chair, next to which is a radiator.

RUTH: (*She is writing the mathematics out on the OHP as she lectures. It is projected onto the top screen.*) ...now you can see what is happening...as x gets larger y will get smaller and we create what is called an asymptote.

Next to the bed, AL begins to dress.

AL: (*Voice-over.*) Hey Ruth, it's me. I went to the passport office to pick up your passport...and of course I can't do that, it's crazy, what were we thinking? Anyway, check this out – they put me in this room for an hour and a half wanting to know why an American, specifically a brown American, wanted to pick up a British passport. It was pretty unpleasant. Anyway it's ready for collection. I love you. Bye.

HARDY watches RAMANUJAN from his desk, far upstage.

HARDY: (*Voice-over.*) You will be sorry to hear that Mr Ramanujan has fallen ill and we are very much alarmed by him. He is a Brahmin and a strict vegetarian. This, in a cold climate, is a terrible difficulty. We discovered that he is not writing to his people, nor hearing from them. He is very reserved about it.

RAMANUJAN: (*Voice-over.*) Now, as well as in the future, I am not in need of anything as I have gained a perfect control over my taste and can live on mere rice with a little salt and lemon juice for an infinite amount of time.

RUTH: And what was interesting to Ramanujan and to me is what happens when you have an infinitesimally small value for x.

AL: (*Voice-over.*) Ruth, I just got back from Hong Kong... I'm trying to make some sense of this list you left me on the kitchen table... OK, so I'm glad you got your passport, but it's a shame you lost it, so I'll look for it. Those books on modular functions you wanted, I found and I'll put them out. I'm kind of worried you are working so much and about this India trip. Can we talk? I love you, bye.

DR WINGFIELD: (*Voice-over.*) The disease with which I am most familiar, tuberculosis, is brought on, or aggravated, by faulty modes of life, which I define as 'overwork, overplay, overworry...'

HARDY: (*Voice-over.*) He has been sent to a hospital near Matlock, in Derbyshire, for a period of recuperation.

RAMANUJAN: (*Voice-over.*) I have been here a month and I have not been allowed fire even for a single day. I have been shivering from cold many a time and I have not been able to take my meals sometimes. After a fortnight of stay they told me...

HARDY: (*Voice-over.*) ...if an integer is O of one, it is zero exactly. If I get any more I will write to you again. I wish you were better and back here – there would be some splendid problems to work at.

RAMANUJAN works, leaning on the radiator.

RAMANUJAN: (*Voice-over.*) The bathrooms are nice and warm. I shall go to the bathroom with pen and paper every day for about an hour and send you two or three papers very soon. In a week or so you may perhaps have a complaint against me from the doctor that I am having bath every day. But I assure you beforehand that I am not going to bathe but to write something.

RUTH: If x is a half, y becomes two. If x is a tenth, y becomes 10. If x is a hundredth, y becomes 100. And we see that as x approaches zero, y gets very big, very quickly and when x reaches zero, the y value shoots right upwards into infinity.

RAMANUJAN: (*Voice-over.*) Last night I had a dream. I imagined the zeta function in my own stomach. When the function reached zero, the singularity shot out an infinite spike. (*A painful burst of music and bright light. RAMANUJAN stands.*) The pain was unbearable.

AL: (*Voice-over.*) Ruth, this India thing is crazy... I'm coming to Brunel. I'll be there in about a half hour. Bye.

HARDY walks downstage and stands next to RAMANUJAN.

HARDY: For my own part I think he may recover completely. I am nervous of trying to rush him: and because we are still having constant mathematical exchanges, I am aware that for the time being I am not an ideal supporter. There is no doubt that any striking recognition now might be a tremendous thing for him. It would make him feel that he was a success, and that it was worthwhile going on trying. I therefore propose S. Ramanujan for a fellowship of the college.

Around them, High Table appears, with FELLOWS seated. HARDY sits.

FELLOW 1: (*Voice-over.*) Master, I have to say this, I'm not having a black man as a fellow of Trinity...

FELLOW 2: (*Voice-over.*) I think it would be highly inappropriate to reject a fellow of the Royal Society.

FELLOW 3: (*Voice-over.*) Can we talk a little of your doubts over his lack of use of proofs...

FELLOW 1: (*Voice-over.*) We thought that was a dirty trick...

FELLOW 3: (*Voice-over.*) Some of his methods are quite unorthodox. Nobody knows how he has arrived at his...

FELLOW 1: (*Voice-over.*) There's actually a rumour that he tried to top himself...

The FELLOWS freeze. HARDY stands. RAMANUJAN climbs onto his chair.

HARDY: Like all Indians he is fatalistic and it is terribly hard to get him to take care of himself. Everyone is frightened of the continual illness and solitude affecting his mind. He has now left the hospital in Matlock and gone to London to rest… I should be visiting him there shortly, as I have been unable to see him now for several weeks…

Suddenly, very loud, the sound of a train, screeching to a halt. The radiator approaches and becomes a train as RAMANUJAN falls in front of it. The lights fade.

(*Voice-over.*) Dear sir, further to our correspondence of the 11th regarding the incident on the underground system, please be assured that my friend and colleague Srinivasa Ramanujan is not only one of the prominent mathematicians of this or any age, but also a fellow of the Royal Society and as such one would hope that any misdemeanour will be overlooked… You should be in no doubt that not only myself, but a number of my colleagues are more than happy to speak on his behalf.

A distant rumble of thunder as RAMANUJAN rolls into the bed.

13

As RUTH continues to silently work at the desk. HARDY walks to the bed, shaking closed an umbrella. The sound of a ticking clock. ANINDA watches them.

ANINDA: Hardy visited him as he lay recuperating in hospital in Putney. Hardy, always inept at introducing a conversation, said, probably without a greeting and certainly as his first remark…

Pause.

HARDY: The number of my taxi-cab was 1729. It seemed to me rather a dull number.

RUTH writes 1729 on the OHP. RAMANUJAN looks at HARDY and then speaks live for the first time:

RAMANUJAN: No, Hardy, 1729 is a very interesting number. It is the smallest number expressible as the sum of two cubes in two different ways.

Pause.

ANINDA: That was the exchange as Hardy recorded it and it must be substantially accurate. He was the most honest of men and, besides, who could possibly have invented it?

Music. HARDY, ANINDA, RAMANUJAN and the bed all move upstage as the walls and whiteboard of the lecture hall slide into position. AL crosses to RUTH at the desk. As he speaks, he picks up the remaining books and packs them away in her boxes.

AL: I've got your books, your ticket and your passport. I can't believe you're going back to India NOW.

RUTH: Come with me, why don't you? Come with me.

AL: I can't come. I have to close this deal. Why do you need to go to India? You don't need to go.

RUTH: I'm 43 years old, Al. Any mathematician of note has done their best work by the time they're 30. I'm not a participant anymore, I'm a spectator.

AL: Write something.

RUTH: I don't want to write anything. I want to feel inspired.

Pause.

AL: What does math give you that I can't?

RUTH: Well, a sense of reality, which is reassuring.

AL: Reality? (*Exploding.*) This is real! This suitcase is real, this box is real! I'm real…that baby was real. (*Beat.*) I'm sorry.

RUTH: That baby was real to me too.

AL: I don't know where that came from. I understand.

RUTH: You don't understand.

AL: I do.

RUTH: (*Looks at him.*) What's the significance of my phone number?

AL: What?

RUTH: (*Angry.*) You see, you don't understand because you haven't even read this fucking book yet!

She pushes the copy of A Mathematician's Apology *towards him, furious. RUTH turns and quickly steps through the board.*

14

AL looks at the book in his hand.

RUTH: (*Voice-over.*) It should be obvious by now that I am only interested in mathematics as a creative art. In that sense it has nothing to do with physical reality. By physical reality, I mean the material world, the world of day and night, earthquakes and eclipses. For me and I suppose for most mathematicians there is another reality, which I shall call mathematical reality.

The rattle of the Chennai train, which we see in silhouette through the screen. AL watches as RUTH collapses and the other passengers surround her. RUTH dies and the image of the train fades.

SURITA: (*Voice-over.*) Mr Al Cooper, you don't know me, my name is Surita Bhogaita. I'm calling from India. I'm somewhere between Chennai and Kumbakonam. (*Pause.*) Erm, listen, can you call me on this number: 07940 715 535... Your wife has been taken ill on the train.

The company enter through the screen. They hold umbrellas. Music. The umbrellas close and HARDY is revealed.

HARDY: There is some of his work about which some mystery still remains. Here I must admit that I am to blame. I suppose that it is always a little difficult for an Englishman and an Indian to understand one another properly, but before he returned to India, I saw Ramanujan almost every day, and could have cleared up most of the obscurity by a bit of cross-examination. I am sorry about this now, but it does not really matter very much, and it was entirely natural. In the first place, I did not know that Ramanujan was going to die.

HARDY walks through the screen and we see RUTH in silhouette, sitting on her chair as if on the train. Music and numbers projected everywhere as the screen flies out. RUTH turns in the chair as she speaks. The company enter and move around her.

RUTH: (*Voice-over.*) For me, and I suppose for most mathematicians, there is another reality, which I shall call mathematical reality. (*Pause.*) Take a chair for example. A chair may be simply a collection of whirling electrons, or an idea in the mind of God; the more we think of it, the fuzzier its outlines become in a haze of sensation which surrounds it. (*Pause.*) But the number 2 or 317 has nothing to do with sensation. 317 is a prime number, not because we think so, or because our minds are shaped in one way rather than another, but because it is so, because mathematical reality is built that way...

The music climaxes and the chair explodes. RUTH and the company dissolve offstage.

15

The light of morning in the lecture hall. AL sleeps on the floor. His phone rings. Eventually he wakes and answers.

AL: Cooper.

DAVID: Al, you should not be picking up. You should be in the air. Where the hell are you? Listen, I need to know when you're getting here. Things just got very big, very quickly. They're biting on call centre closure, relocation, India to the Philippines, immediate implementation, Al!

The CFO is flying in tomorrow, so you have to be here… What flight are you on? Al? Al?

AL closes the phone and puts it back in his pocket. A rattle of keys and the CLEANER enters, switching on the overhead lights. She is talking over her shoulder to someone in Tamil. She turns and sees AL.

CLEANER: (*Astonished.*) What are you still doing here?

AL: Good morning.

The CLEANER stares at him and continues speaking, in Tamil. The roar of a plane overhead and the lecture hall dissolves – the walls and whiteboard disappear. The plane comes together in the middle of the space. AL and ANINDA sit next to each other on the front row. AL has RUTH's red suitcase next to him. Two STEWARDS sit at the back.

CAPTAIN: (*Voice-over.*) Ladies and gentlemen, we are now approaching Madras airport. The fasten seatbelt sign is now illuminated, so please return to your seats and keep your seatbelts fastened for landing. We'll try and get you down gently.

AL has his head in his hands.

ANINDA: You're not feeling well?

AL: I had a rough night.

ANINDA offers AL his hand.

ANINDA: Aninda Rao.

AL: (*Shaking his hand.*) Al Cooper.

ANINDA: You don't live in India?

AL: No, never have. My father left India in 1951.

ANINDA: What do you do?

AL: I work in hedge funds and the futures market. And you?

ANINDA: I'm a Physicist.

AL: Where do you live?

ANINDA: India, Switzerland and London.

AL: (*Grinning.*) We are everywhere, huh? Did you know that
    35.24% of the American software industry is run by
    Indians. I predict that by 2050 India will be the second
    largest economy in the world. Forget about China.

ANINDA: That's a good thing?

AL: Absolutely! The opening of the free market economy in '91
    was the moment India finally broke free from its colonial
    past.

ANINDA: The structures that bind India together are extremely
    fragile and go back millennia. We take them apart at our
    peril.

AL: Come on, Doctor Rao, you're a physicist! You should know
    this: the second law of thermodynamics states that there is
    no construction without destruction.

ANINDA: I believe the second law states that 'the rate of
    change of entropy is always positive', but never mind. Here
    I will quote my Auntie from the *Upanishads*: 'from death
    to death walks a man who does not see everything as being
    connected'. If we cut ourselves off from our past, we will
    have no future.

AL: Do you really believe that?

ANINDA: Do you?

AL: Six months ago I would have said that was bullshit.

ANINDA: And now?

AL: And now... (*Beat.*) I have to go to the bathroom.

> *AL turns and walks upstage. He stands, silhouetted against the projected sky. HARDY rises from the middle of the plane and the light closes in around him. The sky becomes the sea.*

HARDY: He will return to India with a scientific standing and reputation such as no Indian has enjoyed before. I am confident that India will regard him as the treasure he is. His natural simplicity and modesty has never been affected in the least by success. Indeed, all that is wanted is to get him to realise that he really is a success.

CAPTAIN: (*Voice-over.*) We are now descending from a height of 10,000ft... 8,000ft... 6,000ft...

> *Music and the STEWARDS stand. They walk up and down the plane, closing overhead lockers, telling people to fasten their seatbelts, etc. Increasingly, they move in time to the music. They walk upstage and slip off their shoes, turn and begin to dance. The plane dissolves as they dance, faster and faster. AL watches them from upstage. ANINDA walks over to him and together they watch as the STEWARDS transport us to India. AL and ANINDA move downstage and sit on two plastic chairs. The dance climaxes and the STEWARDS exit as Chennai traffic is projected everywhere. The DRIVER enters and they repeat the taxi journey from Scene 1, but with the dialogue muffled by the traffic. They stop and stand in front of the temple.*

RUTH: (*Voice-over.*) Al, it's so beautiful here and hot. I don't understand why you've never come back. I wish you were with me. Madras is incredible. I'm standing in the library, at the window. I'm looking at the sea.

> *A table appears in the centre and AL and ANINDA step into Chennai Library. The LIBRARIAN enters with Ramanujan's notebook. She speaks to AL in Tamil.*

ANINDA: She's saying because the book we want to look at is so fragile, first we'll have to sign here. And also, we cannot take any photographs, photocopies…

AL: OK, thank you.

He signs.

ANINDA: Tell me, what is your interest in Ramanujan?

AL: My wife was obsessed with him. She was a mathematician herself.

ANINDA: Ramanujan is very important to me too! You see, I am a string theorist. We believe that Ramanujan is providing us with the mathematics to support string theory.

AL: Really? (*AL opens the book and RUTH's voice begins to count.*) It's beautiful. What does this mean?

ANINDA: (*Pointing.*) This is what we call a modular function. One only has to observe the physical world for a short period of time, to realise that the laws that govern the very, very large – the stars, galaxies, the entire cosmos – are completely different from the laws that govern the very, very small – the laws that govern the behaviour of the molecules in a strand of hair. The 24 modes in the Ramanujan function correspond to modes of vibration in string theory. In order to protect the original conformal symmetry from being destroyed by quantum theory, a number of highly sophisticated mathematical identities must be satisfied. These identities are precisely the identities satisfied by Ramanujan's modular functions. Look, you see, look here, the term is raised to the 24th power.

AL: I have no idea what you are talking about. But let me try. Are you saying that this math is helping to form a unified vision of the universe?

ANINDA: Yes, it is the holy grail of physics to find a single coherent explanation for the biggest and smallest elements of our universe. To identify the structures which bind everything together.

AL: Did he know this when he was writing it?

ANINDA: I do not believe so. He wrote these during his illness, when he returned from England to India. His body was failing no doubt, but his mind created these beautiful, fragile theorems.

AL: How did he die?

ANINDA: If you really want to know, I will take you to the banks of the Cauvery where he spent much of his time.

RAMANUJAN's voice begins to count down from one hundred. ANINDA and AL exit, moving in time to the counting. Darkness. In the half-light, RAMANUJAN appears and is washed by JANAKI and his MOTHER.

RAMANUJAN: (*Voice-over.*) I am extremely sorry for not writing a single letter to you up to now. I discovered very interesting functions recently, which I call Mock Theta Functions. Unlike the 'False' theta functions, they enter into mathematics as beautifully as the ordinary theta functions. I'm sending you with this letter some examples… If we consider a theta function in transformed Eulerian form for example, $1 +…$

AL and ANINDA stand by the Cauvery River. As ANINDA speaks, we see projected a figure swimming in the water.

ANINDA: This is the Cauvery river. When Ramanujan returned to India from England he came straight away to bathe in the river. The reason being, the God Brahma once had a daughter who was adopted by a man known as Kavera Muni. To show her devotion to her adoptive father she turned herself into a river. All those who now bathe in her are cleansed of their sins.

RAMANUJAN: (*Voice-over.*) …49, 48, 47…

The Cauvery becomes a window at Trinity College and upstage, in the distance, we see HARDY, alone.

HARDY: (*Voice-over.*) (*Over the top of the counting.*) I wish you were better and back here. There will be some splendid problems to work out. At present you must do what the doctors say. However you might be able to think about these things a little; they're very exciting. GHH.

RAMANUJAN: (*Voice-over.*) ...36, 35, 34, 33, 32... (*Over the top of the counting.*) I have a friend who loves me more than all of you, who doesn't want to leave me at all. It's this tuberculosis fever.

RAMANUJAN's MOTHER sings as RAMANUJAN begins to sink to the floor.

HARDY: (*Voice-over.*) Like all Indians, he is fatalistic, and it is terribly hard to get him to take care of himself. Everyone is frightened of the continual illness and solitude affecting his mind.

The light fades on HARDY.

RAMANUJAN: (*Voice-over.*) ...16, 15, 14, 13, 12...

JANAKI: (*Voice-over.*) Early on April 26, 1920, he lapsed into unconsciousness. For two hours I sat with him, feeding him sips of diluted milk.

RAMANUJAN: (*Voice-over.*) ...11, 10, 9, 8, 7, 6, 5, 4, 3, 2...

Silence. Then a low intake of breath. A hard blue light illuminates JANAKI and RAMANUJAN's MOTHER as they throw their hands up in grief and slowly dissolve offstage. Upstage, we again see HARDY's bedroom in Cambridge. As before, GERTRUDE reads from a newspaper.

HARDY: (*Voice-over.*) I still say to myself, when I am depressed or forced to listen to pompous and tiresome people: 'Well, I have done one thing you could never have done, and that is to have collaborated with Ramanujan on something like equal terms.'

RAMANUJAN: (*Voice-over.*) -3, -4, -5, -6...

RUTH: (*Voice-over.*) x plus 1, x plus 2, x plus 3, x plus 4...

Both voices continue.

GERTRUDE: (*She looks down at HARDY.*) Harold? (*She reaches towards him. A moment.*) Oh Harold.

A hard blue light illuminates them for a moment and then fades. Darkness and the Cavery. AL looks at ANINDA.

AL: How old was he when he died?

ANINDA: Ramanujan died just before his 33rd birthday and his colleague GH Hardy died in 1947 at the age of 70 I believe.

A phone rings. Beat.

I think that must be you, no?

AL: Excuse me. (*He finds his phone in his pocket and answers.*) Cooper.

BARBARA: (*Voice-over.*) Hello there Mr Cooper, this is Ms Barbara Jones calling from BT! How are you today?

AL: I'm fine, Barbara Jones.

BARBARA: (*Voice-over.*) I have some very good news for you Mr Cooper! We have finally managed to transfer the number 020 7291 1729 to your name as requested. We got there in the end, eh? Are you pleased Mr Cooper?

Silence.

(*Voice-over.*) Hello?

Silence.

(*Voice-over.*) Hello there Mr Cooper?

AL: Sorry. That was my wife's number – she died.

BARBARA: (*Voice-over.*) (*Quietly.*) I'm very sorry to hear that Mr Cooper.

AL: No, I'm sorry. I don't know why I've said that.

BARBARA: (*Voice-over.*) I'm pleased that we managed to transfer those details for you. This is the last time I will be bothering you. The call centre will be closing down.

AL: You're losing your job?

BARBARA: (*Voice-over.*) Yes, we're all losing our jobs. No more headquarters… 'Back to London', as they say.

AL: I'm really sorry about that. Thank you for everything you've done for me. It meant a lot to me. (*Beat.*) So tell me 'Barbara Jones', what's your name?

BARBARA: (*Voice-over.*) Lakshmi.

AL: Bye, Lakshmi.

BARBARA: (*Voice-over.*) Bye.

He closes the phone, puts it back in his pocket.

ANINDA: I'm so sorry, I couldn't help overhearing. How old was she?

AL: She was 43.

ANINDA: How did she die?

ANINDA gets a packet of cigarettes from his pocket.

AL: She had a brain aneurysm. She died on a train…here in India. (*Beat.*) That's why I came. I had the idea that I would throw her books into the river.

ANINDA offers him the packet.

ANINDA: Maybe have a cigarette before you make such a momentous decision.

AL: (*Taking a cigarette from the packet.*) OK.

They light their cigarettes and begin to smoke them. RUTH appears in the half-light of the river behind them. ANINDA lifts a small urn out of his bag.

ANINDA: I never fail to be surprised by life's symmetries. You see I've brought someone with me as well. This is my Auntie, she died in London, so now I'm bringing her home…

ANINDA's AUNT appears behind them.

AL: You took her on the plane?

ANINDA: Yes…she got a free ride. (*Beat.*) And now I'm going to put her into the river and say my last words to her. Although really, I'm always talking to her.

AL: On the other side of infinity.

ANINDA: (*Correcting him.*) On the same line.

The company, headed by RUTH and ANINDA's AUNT, form a diagonal line across the stage. They look at AL.

AL: Yeah. You know what? I have a piece of my wife's chalk. I'll put that in the river instead.

AL looks at the piece of chalk. RUTH touches his shoulder.

RUTH: (*Voice-over.*) Al, you know that box of mine with all that stuff and inside you found a piece of chalk. Do you know now why it was there? I want to read you this… (*The company spread across the stage, each in their own small pool of light. ANINDA pours his AUNT's ashes into the river and each member of the company pours salt.*) 'What reconciles me to my own death more than anything else is the image of a place: a place where your bones and mine are buried, thrown, uncovered together. They are strewn there pell-mell. One of your ribs leans against my skull. A metacarpal of my left hand lies inside your pelvis. (Against my broken ribs your breast like a flower.) (*AL places the chalk on the floor in front of him.*) The hundred bones of our feet are scattered like gravel. It is strange that this image of our proximity, concerning as it does mere phosphate of calcium, should bestow a sense of peace. Yet it does. With you I can imagine a place where to be phosphate of calcium is enough.'

Very slowly, light begins to fade on each member of the company. As it fades, AL and ANINDA stand and lift their cigarettes to their mouths. RUTH's voice begins to count up from 1…

THE END.

Appendix

The functional equation of the Riemann zeta function

$$2^{1-z}\Gamma(z)\zeta(z)\cos(\frac{1}{2}\pi z) = \pi^z\zeta(1-z)$$

where $z = x + iy$, $\quad i = \sqrt{-1}$

$$\Gamma(z) = \int_0^\infty e^{-t}t^{z-1}dt = (z-1)!$$

$$\zeta(z) = \sum_{n=1}^\infty \frac{1}{n^z}$$

$\Rightarrow$ real value of 2, $\quad \zeta(2) = \frac{\pi^2}{6}$ (known result)

$$2^{1-2}\,\Gamma(2)\,\zeta(2)\,\cos(\frac{1}{2}2\pi) = \pi^2\,\zeta(1-2)$$

$$\therefore\ 2^{-1}\cdot(2-1)!\cdot\frac{\pi^2}{6}\cdot\cos\pi = \pi^2\,\zeta(-1)$$

$$\therefore\ \frac{1}{2}\cdot 1\cdot\frac{\pi^2}{6}\cdot -1 = \pi^2\,\zeta(-1)$$

$$\therefore\ \zeta(-1) = -\frac{1}{12}$$

$$\therefore\ \frac{1}{1^{-1}} + \frac{1}{2^{-1}} + \frac{1}{3^{-1}} + \frac{1}{4^{-1}} + \frac{1}{5^{-1}} + \ldots = -\frac{1}{12}$$

$$\therefore\ \frac{1}{1} + \frac{1}{1/2} + \frac{1}{1/3} + \frac{1}{1/4} + \frac{1}{1/5} + \ldots = -\frac{1}{12}$$

$$\therefore\ 1 + 2 + 3 + 4 + 5 + \ldots = -\frac{1}{12}$$